to all gentleness
WILLIAM
CARLOS WILLIAMS
the Doctor Poet

FOREWORD BY WILLIAM ERIC WILLIAMS, M.D.

NEW PREFACE BY THE AUTHOR

NEIL BALDWIN

INPRINT
EDITIONS

Black Classic Press
Baltimore

First Paperback Edition
Published 2008
Inprint Editions

Library of Congress Control Number: 2007941001

ISBN 13: 9781580730389
ISBN 10: 1580730388

Cover photo: Eve Arnold/Magnum

Author photo: Allegra Baldwin

Cover design: Kamau Sennaar

Printed by BCP Digital Printing,
an affiliate company of Black Classic Press

ALSO BY NEIL BALDWIN

The American Revelation:
Ten Ideals That Shaped Our Country
From the Puritans to the Cold War

National Book Award Classics:
Essays Celebrating Our Literary Heritage

Henry Ford and the Jews:
The Mass Production of Hate

Legends of the Plumed Serpent:
Biography of a Mexican God

Edison: Inventing the Century

Man Ray: American Artist

The Poetry Writing Handbook

On the Trail of Messages (poems)

The Writing Life (co-editor)

The Manuscripts & Letters of William Carlos Williams in the
Poetry Collection, Lockwood Memorial Library, SUNY/Buffalo:
A Descriptive Catalogue (co-author). Preface by Robert Creeley.

PREFACE

William Carlos Williams - the poet for today

"...sure not all
Those melodies sung into the world's ear
Are useless: sure a poet is a sage;
A humanist, physician to all men."
    —John Keats, *The Fall of Hyperion: A Dream* (Summer, 1819)

"...unless a man uses his authority for others, to make himself a
servant in some sense for humanity, to man, to those about him
who need him—he turns out to be a selfish bastard."
    —William Carlos Williams, Letter to Robert McAlmon
    (February 23, 1944)

       *   *   *

My expressed intention in writing this new Preface for *To All
Gentleness* so long after its original publication was to bring William
Carlos Williams forward into the twenty-first century for a new
generation of readers.

Now I'm thinking this sounds somewhat pretentious.

Who am I to assume such a mission? Surely this native
giant, "WCW"—tough yet tender poet of Jersey, house-calling
pediatrician, cultural icon and *iconoclast*, beloved patron saint of the
Beats, resolute homegrown American, champion of street-speech
as raw material for verse—requires no such resurrection. Surely

dozens of books by the determined poet who declared at the age of sixty-five that "No defeat is made up entirely of defeat—since/ the world it opens is always a place/formerly/unsuspected" will survive on their own legs.

And yet...and yet...stick with me through this brief essay as I share some reminiscences and revelations, which have brought Williams, reborn, back into my *own* affections.

In the early spring of 1982, when I started to write the book you now hold in your hands, my wife, Roberta, and I were trying to make a decent living as freelance journalists, both working at home in a prewar, two-bedroom apartment in Brooklyn Heights, one block from the Promenade. Our son, Nicholas, had just turned three years old; our daughter, Allegra, barely nine months. Afternoons, the babysitter was supposed to keep the children occupied in their cramped playroom at the other end of the apartment near the kitchen while Roberta and I took refuge in the master bedroom and pounded away at separate typewriters. Sooner or later, inevitably, Nicholas wrestled free, scampered across the living room, and began to bang on our door with his little fists, screaming at the top of his lungs; and then a gust of wind from the East River would push across the window sill, scattering onto the floor un-numbered draft manuscript pages I had carefully laid out in sequence on the bed, having no other place to arrange them.

Thus proceeded my first unruly lesson in the arduous and messy interpenetration of life and work.

Flash-forward to the past six months here on the top floor of our spacious stucco Tudor in the leafy suburbs. The quiet study under the eaves where I retreat to write overlooks a broad, sylvan backyard, maple trees whispering subtly after a pre-dawn rain. I've been making repeated forays to the hallway outside my private chamber to scan several sagging shelves of well-thumbed New Directions paperbacks by WCW—poems, naturally, both collected and selected; as well as plays; short fiction, including one entire volume of "doctor stories" (he delivered more than three thousand babies); book reviews on American literature and essays on modernist culture; four novels; interviews; letters; and *Paterson*, the long poem that was his troubled, incomplete epic labor over four decades.

In the intervening years since *To All Gentleness* was published, I have gone on to write books of biography, history, and fiction, extending my intellectual reach far afield from its original grounding in American poetry. These additional titles rose up like a dense mental wall further separating me from WCW. In a nervous, necessary effort to reconnect—in order to write about him again after such long silence—I decided to re-read my way through Williams' entire corpus of poetry in chronological order, beginning with the 1909 pamphlet of juvenilia he had printed himself and sold at the corner stationery store in Rutherford, and ending with the final fragmentary 1961 notes for a projected *Paterson* Book VI found among his papers after his death.

To my surprise and relief, this tentative and, as I say, apprehensive exercise in literary reacquaintance turned out to be the easy and pleasurable awakening of a dormant friendship, starting with the earliest section of the two-volume *Collected Poems*. Pages flew by as I smiled and nodded familiarly at WCW's romantic efforts, archaic diction reflecting his initial infatuation with John Keats, as when "I must read a lady poesy/The while we glide by many a leafy bay,/Hid deep in rushes, where at random play/The glossy black winged May-flies..." His Keatsian affinity went deeper than narrative poetic style and meter; for the young Keats had likewise studied hard to enter the medical profession in London, only to abandon that metier for what turned out to be an itinerant, penniless, and tragically truncated life consecrated to literature alone.

William Carlos Williams' great stylistic shift into characteristic, breath-driven *enjambment* arrived about the time he turned thirty ("First he said:/It is the woman in us/That makes us write—/Let us acknowledge it—"); soon thereafter came the pediatrician's snapshot observations of children, like the little girl who "hides herself/in the full sunlight/her cordy legs writhing/beneath the little flowered dress;" and the empathy with signs in nature as immediately transcribed reflections of his mercurial mood, as when the poet observes how, among "the half-stripped trees...the leaves flutter drily/and refuse to let go," or he senses, driving his car to work, "By the road to the contagious hospital/under the surge of the blue/mottled clouds driven from the/northeast— a cold wind."

All these insights came back to me in a delightful rush—the way Dr. Williams, returning home dead-tired after visiting "the houses of the very poor," grabbed a moment to scribble on a scrap of prescription pad "in the darkness/through the broom of branches—," and ask himself wryly "What are black 4 a.m.'s after all but black/4 a.m.'s like anything else," pushing beyond the fatigue that would have driven any typical poet straight to bed, dredging up the imagination required to appreciate "Vistas/of delight waking suddenly/before a cheated world."

I marveled again at Williams' indomitable spirit and relentless self-goading persistence into the difficult stretches when he could not compose and felt like "a sick man/and want[ed] to die...We have written," he conceded, "but not enough/not intensely enough--/We have not carried/the same construction/far enough/nowhere near far enough."

I remembered the long-suffering wait for academic and establishment recognition that allied WCW with the fishermen he observed from a distance leaning over a bridge, who could not "catch anything/more than quietness, to the formal/rhythms of casting—that slow dance;" and, likewise, his identification with the shirtless trench laborer down the block, having "no aversion to taking/his spade to the head/of any who would derogate/his performance in the craft."

Indeed, work for Williams was all of a kind, whether drawing a past-term emergency baby forth by forceps and having to break its clavicle in the process; typing out twenty drafts of a three-stanza poem over and over again until it marched down the page just right; or, at the age of fifty-nine, carrying "a tar bucket and a stick," clambering to the roof of the three-story wood frame house where he lived for half a century to fix some leaks, "by way of one of the gutters…straddling the peak and looking around."

My late and much-missed mentor, Robert Creeley, his constant debt to Williams freely acknowledged, observed in his Introduction to my *Catalogue of Williams Manuscripts at the University of Buffalo* that "the virtue of what Williams wrote is equal to the virtue of the diverse flowering earth he loved. Both change endlessly, to remain the same." Delving into quotidian life, Williams transcended that world in artfully utilitarian fashion, embedding into poetry his resultant impressions, what he called "the particulars, the radiant gist." He speculated, in the *denouement* of his career, "Are facts not flowers/and flowers facts/or poems flowers/or all works of the imagination,/interchangeable?"—no matter, I interject herewith, if they be made up of molecules; seeds; typewritten sheets; or even, nowadays, arrays of pixels.

If I must therefore select one salient dimension of this massive textual and emotional legacy, it would be William Carlos Williams' continued ability to speak to me—hopefully, to all of us—from his distant time of localized obsession with concrete, "pure products of America" all the way into our digitized, placeless, virtual era. His beloved "particulars" have become infinitesimally smaller nowadays, but still contain as much power to move us, if we know how, when—and where—to look.

I urge you, reader, to forge ahead inspired by that visionary spirit.

Neil Baldwin,
2008

To All Gentleness:

WILLIAM CARLOS WILLIAMS

The Doctor-Poet

To All Gentleness:

WILLIAM CARLOS WILLIAMS

The Doctor-Poet

by NEIL BALDWIN

WITH A FOREWORD BY WILLIAM ERIC WILLIAMS, M.D.

ATHENEUM · NEW YORK · 1984

LIBRARY OF CONGRESS CATALOGING IN PUBLICATION DATA

Baldwin, Neil   To all gentleness.

SUMMARY: *A biography of a man who successfully combined
two careers as a family physician and as a poet.*
*1. Williams, William Carlos, 1883–1963—Juvenile
literature.   2. Poets, American—20th century—Biography—
Juvenile literature.   3. Physicians—United States—
Biography—Juvenile literature.   [1. Williams, William
Carlos, 1883–1963.   2. Poets, American.   3. Physicians]
I. Title.*
PS3545.I544Z574   1984   811'.52 [B] [92]   83-15625
ISBN 0-689-31030-7

*Grateful acknowledgement is given to New Directions Publishing
Corporation for permission to reprint from the following works
of William Carlos Williams, Ezra Pound, and H.D.*

A Recognizable Image: William Carlos Williams on Art and Artists.
Copyright © 1939, 1954, 1962 by William Carlos Williams.

Selected Essays of William Carlos Williams. Copyright © 1931,
1936, 1938, 1939, 1949, 1942, 1946, 1948, 1949, 1951, 1954 by
William Carlos Williams.

Selected Letters of William Carlos Williams. Copyright © 1957 by
William Carlos Williams.

For ROBERTA

a profusion
of pink roses bending ragged in the rain—
speaks to me of all gentleness and its
enduring.

—WILLIAM CARLOS WILLIAMS,
To All Gentleness, 1944.

ACKNOWLEDGMENTS

This book could not have been written without the generous help of William Carlos Williams's two sons.

William Eric Williams, M.D., invited me out to visit Nine Ridge Road in Rutherford, New Jersey, where he lives and practices medicine, just as his father did before him. He patiently answered my numerous questions, and we sifted through hundreds of family photographs together. Several of them are published for the first time in this book.

Paul Herman Williams and I spent a couple of mornings talking in his Rutherford home, just a few blocks away from his older brother's, and he reminisced openly and honestly about his childhood. He also took the time to take me on a guided tour of the town and environs, pointing out important streets and landmarks. We visited his father's grave together.

I continue to be grateful to James Laughlin, publisher of New Directions Books, and William Carlos Williams's long-time friend and editor. I first met Mr. Laughlin ten years ago, when I compiled a catalogue of Williams's manuscripts, and he has always been supportive of my work in the field. His recollections of Williams in the early years of their friendship added much to the shape of this biography.

Kenneth Burke met Williams sixty years ago, and understands the man and his poetry better than just about anyone. We spent a long afternoon of conversation in his back yard at Andover, New Jersey, and I am grateful for his sharp and humorous perspective.

In his own fine poems, Robert Creeley clearly exemplifies the Williams legacy for the generation of writers following him, and he has been an unfailingly generous standard for us. I am pleased to have his recollections of Williams included here, the result of a wide-ranging interview.

Thanks, also, to Bill Higginson, a younger poet of New Jersey, for a fascinating trip around Paterson and Garret Mountain Park one lovely day in the spring; to Edith Heal Berrien, for her remembrances of Williams and Flossie; to Robert Coles, M.D., for his perspective on Williams as physician and social commentator; and to poets David Ignatow and Joel Oppenheimer, for their valuable, first-hand accounts and intelligent perceptions of Williams as influence.

Three biographers have followed the Williams trail in the past fifteen years. The excellent pioneering work accomplished by Mike Weaver, Reed Whittemore, and Paul Mariani made my progress much less difficult.

The editorial staff at New Directions Publishing Corporation were always ready with quick facts over the phone, photographs, permissions forms, and generally high-spirited help: Daniel Allman, Peggy Fox, Peter Glassgold, and Griselda Ohannessian.

For assistance with archival material, including tape recordings, access to literary manuscripts, and photographs, I am grateful to Gladys Eckardt, director, Bernice Reed, and the staff of the Rutherford Free Public Library; Dr. Robert Bertholf, curator, Beatrice Horton, and the student staff at the Poetry/ Rare Books Collection, University Library, State University of New York at Buffalo; Dr. Neda M. Westlake, curator, Rare Book Collection, Charles Patterson van Pelt Library, University of Pennsylvania; Linda Lawson, Photographic Library, Metropolitan Museum of Art, New York City; Sylvie Rebbot, Magnum Photos, Inc., New York City; and Gerald S. Lestz, president, Charles Demuth Foundation, Lancaster, Pennsylvania.

It is certainly true that a writer must do his work of writing in solitude. But the task of putting this book together was made considerably less arduous by the advice, support, and understanding of family, friends, and colleagues: David S. Baldwin, M.D., Halee Baldwin, Patricia Bosworth, Tom Bridwell, Bonnie Chapin, Richard Huttner, Suzanne Jasper, Madeleine Keller, Geoff Keller, Pam Keller, Marilyn Kitchell, Jay Laghi, Marcia Marshall, Francis V. O'Connor, Jonathan Plutzik, Beatrice de Regniers, Janice S. Robinson, Emily M. Wallace, and Jeannie Williams.

Special thanks to the enthusiastic students in my Fall semester 1982 New School for Social Research seminar on Williams, Pound, Marianne Moore, and H.D. Many of the themes in this book were clarified through their responses to the poetry we read together.

And finally, for my wife, Roberta, and my children,

Nicholas and Allegra, there are no words that seem right. For a year and more, this book drew me farther away from them than I wished to go. Their constancy gave me the strength to move forward.

N.B.
Brooklyn Heights
Winter, 1983

CONTENTS

FOREWORD

It is interesting and appropriate that Neil Baldwin has addressed himself to students, the younger generations. William Carlos Williams himself found his best audience among the youthful. He was a rebel, not of the establishment. He was figuratively "drummed out of the corps" by the "in" group at the conservative universities and by the accepted critics and writers who were being published. So it was with amazement that I overheard a conversation at lunch between exams in the spring of 1934. One of the seniors was airing a complaint about a question on his final written exam in English. "Who the hell is William Carlos Williams?" Little did I suspect that my father's poetry was becoming recognized by academia. I must confess I was as taken aback as was my indignant fraternity brother that Dad's work had somehow infiltrated this remote Berkshire valley. Today hardly a week passes that some undergraduate doesn't seek me out to winnow pearls from my expositions concerning him.

One of Williams's characteristics was his chauvinism, his love of the United States of America. And I have never found this easy to explain, because neither of his parents ever thought enough of America to bother to take out citizenship papers. The common language in his home when he was a growing boy was Spanish. The family diet, mores, expletives, heroes and manner of dress were anything but American. On the other hand his familiars in the community, the children of the Hyslops, Alyeas, Browns, Armstrongs and Livingstons were all as American as baked beans and apple pie, natives of this land for generations, not an immigrant in the lot. Was he ingested and branded by the herd? What American kid wants to be known as a "furriner"? The apparent normalcy of these Anglo-Saxon households, compared to *his* house where there was a nutty uncle, little English spoken, and a parade of Spanish- and French-speaking foreign visitors inconveniencing the domestic routine served, I'm sure, to reinforce his allegiance to his American friends. It wasn't until years later that under the aegis of his medical degree he would gain entry to these local homes, and appreciate the Freudian squirmings, posturing and conflicts that were concealed behind their walls. But the die had been cast. The tiger wouldn't change his stripes. After all he was a native-born American Boy.

He would reject the foreign manners and mores, but when he left home he would take with him two things: the emotional temperament and love of the arts of his mother, and the intelligence and energy of his father. These were the tools he would employ in painting his American scene, but using an entirely new idiom, discarding the molds of the English versifiers, and the hackneyed phrases and clauses of the traditional poet. America was too big to fit in any mold. America was young, dynamic, evolving; how stultifying to employ the traditional forms in ANY of the arts to create an American image. The forms must be new, mint, unprecedented, virgin; and the search for these forms would be his goal for the rest of his life. The academicians would not be impressed. Recognition and honors would be slow coming. But the young intellectuals would keep his name alive and carry on in his tradition when he was gone. James Laughlin in Boston, later founder of New Directions Publishers, his unquestioning publisher and friend for the last thirty years of his life; Reed Whittemore in New Haven, later to become Flossie's choice to write his biography; Louis Zukofsky in Brooklyn, his most devoted editor and critic to the bitter end; all these and more would testify to his worth.

As a teenager my father had vowed to be perfect, never to lie, and come what may, always to tell the truth. As a medical student he decided that ". . . medicine, a job I enjoyed, would make it possible to live and write as I wanted to." He would be "normal, undrunk, balanced in everything." As a young physician traveling through Europe and attending the Comédie Française, he found the presentation of *Le Monde ou l'on S'ennuie* ". . . remote, stilted, completely artificial." He concluded about the French theatre, "To them the meaning of art is skill, to manipulate the parts to produce an effect diametrically opposed to my own values . . ." In a letter to his mother in 1917, he would recall that he had, while at the University of Pennsylvania, given up medicine for poetry. His life's work was poetry, his avocation medicine. He had his heroes and models in the arts, from Shakespeare to Whitman among the poets, Beethoven to Gershwin among the musicians, and Breughel to Demuth among the painters. He would be touched by them all, but his ultimate style and idiom would be his own. Nothing stilted, no lies, everything normal and "undrunk." Poetry became his addiction, his "habit," the gyroscope that held him on an even keel when the going got rough. He found poetry everywhere. No need to search, just keep the receptors uncluttered and let it come to you. Get it down while it's hot. No garble, no distortion, and nothing artificial. I'm sure he was familiar with the old orthopedic adage "Splint 'em where they lie!" To the physician it means to immobilize the fracture before the patient or some well-meaning Samaritan damages the injured part further. He would practice this in his poetry. When an old woman takes a plum from a wrinkled paper bag and relishes its flavor and juiciness, *say so*! When a cat climbs over a jam closet putting its paws precisely and rhythmically into some clay pots, *say so*! If some bawdy dancers with big cans, hips and breasts shake the joint as they go 'round and 'round and 'round, *say so*! And he did!

He was a capable and respected physician. He was an accurate and honest reporter in his poetry. The trained observer physician complemented the vibrant imagist in the poet. Either occupation for most men would be a full-time job. Fortunately he had at hand an inexhaustible well of energy that made it possible to do both jobs well.

The doctor nurtured the poet through his privileged admission into the lives of his patients. The poet returned into the physician the distillate of his observations, making the doctor a more humane and altruistic ministrant to the sick. But it was a lonely existence, I suspect. There was little time or energy left once the poet and physician had been sated. He was exploring new frontiers and the frontier is always scantily populated. He was overthrowing, or attempting to overthrow, tradition. Like a wild stallion, he took the bit in his teeth, kicked over the traces and galloped for the horizon. Who can relate to a wild stallion? Who wants to? Perhaps Neil Baldwin's word picture will bring him, if not into the stable, at least into the barnyard where we can study at our leisure his good and bad points.

William Eric Williams, M.D.

INTRODUCTION

It was a spring morning in my tenth grade year at Horace Mann, when I first discovered William Carlos Williams. The country day school campus perched high on a hilltop in Riverdale—an hour's bus and subway ride from a different world, my home in Manhattan—looked more lovely than ever.

Flowers in full bloom surrounding the athletic field gleamed in early morning sun. The diamond was ready for that afternoon's ball game, basepaths laid out neatly in white, pitcher's mound newly raked. The brown, tree-shrouded hills and dusty green fields of Van Cortlandt Park far below reminded me that cross-country track season would be starting in just a few months. I'd be captain of the Varsity squad in my junior year, would have to run even faster to keep my teammates' respect.

In fact, I *was* running, running down a corridor toward the school library to catch some last-minute studying, my blazer open, tie flying wildly over my shoulder, elbowing past the other boys. Suddenly, in front of the exhibit cases to the left of the library entrance, I skidded to a halt. In those days, it was the custom at H.M. to display the works of distinguished alumni authors. "William Carlos Williams, 1883–1963," the sign behind the sliding glass panels read, "Class of 1902." A photograph of a gray-haired man peered out at me. I immediately noticed his eyes, so large, so penetrating; and his mouth, ever-so-slightly smiling, a gentle expression hovering somewhere between wistful and amused.

I had never seen so many books by one writer in one place before. Why, there must have been at least thirty or forty volumes. Winner of the Pulitzer Prize for Poetry, the Bollingen Prize, and the Gold Medal for Poetry of the

National Institute of Arts and Letters. And he was a *doctor*, too? I couldn't believe it.

I peered into the display case more closely: Williams was born in Rutherford, New Jersey; attended Horace Mann for three years, 1899–1902 ("That's quite a journey, every day," I thought; then remembered, of course, that was when the campus was downtown, at Columbia University); on the track team while at school (I smiled, feeling proud of him, of myself—so we had something in common!); also schooled in Switzerland and France, then went to medical school at the University of Pennsylvania.

Williams was a practicing physician specializing in family medicine and obstretrics in his home town for over forty years, delivering by his own count more than three thousand babies. He was the author of plays, novels, short stories, essays, an autobiography, and hundreds of poems, including the epic *Paterson*.

The bell rang, catching me by surprise. Reluctantly, I turned away, trudged up the stairs to my first-period class, promising myself that some day I would have to look further into the life of this remarkable and talented man.

◆◆

At college, however, *he* found *me*.

I wanted to be a history major, as yet harbored no thoughts of poetry or literature, innocently insisted that boundary lines between subjects had to be preserved, until a friend handed me a copy of *In the American Grain*, by none other than William Carlos Williams, published 1925. A poet had tackled history, and succeeded.

In the book, Williams expressed pride at being an American, first and foremost, by painting admiring portraits of our past heroes: Christopher Columbus, the Pilgrims, Daniel Boone, George Washington, Benjamin Franklin, John Paul Jones, Abraham Lincoln, and others. He combined the use of their own words and writings with his vivid imagination, interpreting the past in a unique way. What *is* our America, after all, Williams seemed to conclude, if not a place where newness comes into its own, time and time again? What *is* America, if not a place where explorers and discoverers in all fields have always been honored?

❧

In graduate school at Buffalo, working toward a Ph.D. in English, I lived truly on my own. I spent many hours alone. I did a lot of hard thinking. I discovered poetry, and began to study it, publish it, teach it, live and breathe it, and most important of all, I began to *write* it.

And William Carlos Williams caught up with me yet again.

During the 1930s, 40s, and 50s, he had donated thousands of manuscript pages—handwritten and typed drafts for published work of all kinds, poetry and prose—to the Lockwood Library Poetry Collection at the University of Buffalo. The papers remained filed away in a temperature-controlled, room-sized vault, available only to scholars with time and interest to sift through them.

The chairman of the English department at Buffalo, Prof. Marcus Klein, and the Director Emeritus of the Library, Dr. Oscar Silverman, asked fellow graduate student Steven Meyers and me if we would be interested in compiling a catalogue of all the Williams papers so that the huge collection might become more widely known and more easily researched. The catalogue would be our doctoral dissertation.

After some fears about the task that lay before us, we agreed. And I will never forget the first time I held in my hands the actual worksheet for a poem by William Carlos Williams.

The paper was yellow, fragile to the touch, turning slightly orange with age at the edges. The words had been typed with great force; I turned the sheet over and could see impressions coming through the back. In some places, the letters "o" and "a", the paper was ripped from the typewriter keys' impact. The poem itself, perhaps three or four stanzas, was almost entirely covered over by hand-written corrections in blue ink, black ink, and red and blue colored pencil. Lines had been drawn every which way, words crossed out, replaced, moved around from one stanza to the next—all with great speed and precision in a practically unreadable scribble.

Over the following three years, my friend Steven Meyers and I sat side by side at a long, oak table in the Poetry Collection reading room and organized each and every scrap of paper in the Williams archive, more than twenty thousand sheets in all. And we discovered the same hard work and care in every manuscript.

ﻫﺟ

Before and since the publication of our catalogue by G. K. Hall and Company in 1978, I've written many essays on Williams's life and work.

And still, I ask the question, "Who *was* William Carlos Williams?" Who is he now, to me, as memory and time cloud the twenty years since his death, the twenty years since I saw his photograph in a bookcase?

He was a man who believed in the importance of little things in daily life: the call of a bird, the cry of a new-born baby, the flash of a traffic light, a flower in bloom; a woman's laugh, the swish of her skirt as she walked past; a friend's welcome letter after long silence; the way tree-tops caught the first light of dawn; the way a river's rippled surface caught the last light of dusk.

He believed that the local world closest to us, the street where we live, the town where we grow up, the people we love, family, friends, parents, children—was the world that belonged in poems. He shrugged off complaints of other writers who said they had nothing important to write about. Nonsense, he told them. Open your eyes, clean out your ears, it's all there, *right in front of you!*

He believed that if a task was important enough and worth doing enough, time could be found to do it, no matter how busy you might be. In Williams's life, that meant two activities: medicine and poetry. He was never too busy with his patients to abandon the craft of poetry. He was never too busy with his writing to ignore the complaints of the sick and dying.

He was a man ruled by his emotions. To feel something deeply—whether it was the strength of a newly discovered word that fit, just so, into a troublesome line of verse, or a mother's burst of joy when her baby finally arrived after a difficult, painful labor—those passions made life worthwhile.

He was a driven man, who thought nothing of staying out all night on a maternity case, taking a few nips of home-brewed whiskey and drinking a toast with the happy new father, driving home in the darkness, bounding up the stairs, shedding his clothes—only to churn out ten pages of a short story before falling exhausted and practically unconscious into bed a scant hour before daybreak.

Despite affliction after affliction in the last years of his life, despite a heart attack, hernias, cancer, and a series of strokes that left him nearly blind, Williams pushed himself again and again to the typewriter, plugging away on the trail of yet another perfect poem.

William Carlos Williams led a life of contradictions. Despite his many achievements, he had doubts. He spoke often—in letters to close friends and in some of his best poems—of feeling lonely, isolated and cut off from society. Yet, to the people of his town, he was the popular, available, skilled and generous country doctor who always had an hour to spare for one more house call. He pledged himself from childhood to write the truth as he saw it, and chose poetry especially because it was impossible to lie and still compose a good poem. Yet, he often despaired of an author's life when, try as he might, writing honestly as he knew how, no one seemed to pay any attention to him. And although Williams often proclaimed his love for Flossie, his wife of fifty years, he also sought romantic involvement elsewhere; his wandering eye for other women was never at rest.

His longtime friend and publisher, James Laughlin, says that Williams placed so much faith in the power of words, he believed that the right use of language could change the world.

To his friend Kenneth Burke, looking back over sixty years, Williams was above all else a *sincere* man. His passion for language made him straight-speaking, direct, and honest.

Williams's elder son, William Eric, also a doctor, marvels to this day at his father's endless energy, and still cannot explain where it came from. Williams's younger son, Paul, remembers his father as a stubborn person with a firm sense of right and wrong, a fiercely moral individual who would fight until his dying day for a principle he believed worth defending, in poetry or any other field.

ও§

William Carlos Williams insisted that "the artist is always and forever painting only one thing: a self-portrait."

Williams's emotional face is presented in all of his poems. That is why you will find so many of them in my book. His poetry is like a beautiful thread spinning and unraveling from his first awkward experiment with verse in high school, to the last majestic love poems of old age. His life is written in his poems for us to trace.

Williams also insisted that "all writing starts and ends with poetry;" and so it has been my responsibility as a biographer to follow closely the path of poetic truth through the complicated life of a very active, endlessly working writer and physician, and to come up with my *own* portrait of him. Many rich colors were available for my palette, more than I ever dreamed would be when I began to write this book.

This is indeed a book of facts—many, many facts—as any biography should be; and equally a book of imagination about an American hero.

Neil Baldwin

To All Gentleness:

WILLIAM CARLOS WILLIAMS

The Doctor-Poet

I

"The alphabet of the trees"

Willie Williams peered with excitement through the slats in the fence bordering his back yard.

The shimmering, magical green forest beckoned. Spring held out its promise, had always been the little boy's favorite season and always would be; a time of renewal, a time when trees once again became places to hide from his mother, or whoever might come looking for him.

Willie took a deep breath, vaulted over the fence into neighbor Peter Kip's property, and climbed the leafiest chestnut tree he could find, deep in that forbidden forest behind his home on West Passaic Avenue in the small, parklike town of Rutherford, New Jersey.

Mr. Kip's farm—rye, corn, potato fields, and apple orchards—had been flourishing for more than one hundred and fifty years. The main house, 138 Union Avenue, was built before 1720, and people said George Washington actually slept there during the Revolutionary War. A fragrant wisteria vine twisted around the latticed well house. Nearby, flowers grew wild. Willie Williams was proud he knew the name of each and every one: anemone, star of Bethlehem, brilliant wild geranium, hepatica, tulip, and his favorite, the spiky purple violet.

Kip's forest was Willie's personal wild world, a place

3

to retreat, most of the time alone, sometimes with best friend Jim Hyslop, away from noisy gangs of other kids. When Willie grew up, he wanted to be a forester, to make his living caring for trees all year round. A sensitive, fragile child, terrified of thunder and lightning and most of all of the dark, he liked nothing better than to wander and explore the green landscape of rural Rutherford. There was so much to be learned, so much inspiration to be found in nature.

⋙

William Carlos Williams was born in Rutherford on September 17, 1883. At that time, it was a country town of one square mile, with a population of less than three thousand. It had no sewers, water supply, gas, or electricity. A quiet, sleepy kind of place, the loudest sound was the clop, clop, clop of horse-drawn carriages over primitive streets made from simple wooden planks laid down over bare earth. Flowers pushed their way up between the boards, and on hot summer days, yellowjackets buzzed forth from mud nests under the makeshift sidewalks.

Willie and his friends could buy candy for a penny on Park Avenue, the town's main thoroughfare. Then they would be off to Berry's Creek for a swim, or a game of baseball, or perhaps a hike along the railroad tracks to explore an abandoned copper mine, or down to the ferry landing on the nearby Passaic River, to watch a colorful sailing regatta. There was lively passenger boat service, too, between Rutherford and Newark, the big city seven miles downstream. From there, you could catch another boat to the biggest city of them all, New York, just across the Hudson River.

Rutherford had expanded greatly during the Civil War, when many European immigrants had come to settle in the area, but much of the center of town in Willie's day remained woodland. Vast green meadowlands stretched all around, a natural playground for the children, bordered by white violets and cattails, and full of wildlife: crabs, fish of all varieties, and turtles in shadowy swamps; and muskrat, deer, egret, wild quail, woodcocks, and Canada geese.

Over his entire life, William Carlos Williams observed Rutherford's slow and steady changes. After he was married, in 1913, Williams moved into a house at Nine Ridge Road, right near the center of town, just half a mile from where he was born; and he died in that same house fifty years later.

Rutherford was too close to the hustle and bustle of New York City to remain completely untouched by suburban expansion. Williams took satisfaction in the fact that if he stood on the eastern edge of town in later years he could make out the city skyline still safely at a distance, a place he reached in a half-hour's drive. That was the appropriate distance from midtown, nine miles west: near enough to urban civilization to take advantage of it when he wanted to, in small doses, and far enough to enjoy the hushed silence of dawn in the country.

Williams, and his younger brother, Edgar, born thirteen months after him, were sons of immigrant parents. He was always proud of his melting-pot background: "Of mixed ancestry, I felt from earliest childhood that America was the only home I could ever possibly call my own," he wrote, "I felt it was expressly founded for me, personally."

Willie's father, William George Williams, was born in Birmingham, England, in 1851, and came first to New York City as a boy of five with his single mother, Emily Dickenson. There, she married Benjamin Wellcome, a photographer, and they moved to St. Thomas, Virgin Islands, where William George grew up. As a young man, he worked for the company of Lanman and Kemp, producers of "Florida Water," a cologne. He met his future wife, Raquel Helene Rose Hoheb, who was Puerto-Rican born of

French, Dutch, Spanish, and Jewish descent, in Puerto Plata. The couple moved to New York City, where they were married in 1882; then to Jersey City; and finally settled in Rutherford. William George Williams worked as a district manager and salesman for Lanman and Kemp until his death in 1918. For thirty-five years, he commuted every day into New York City from Rutherford.

Despite his emigration at such a tender age, William George Williams was an Englishman through and through, a restrained gentleman behind his well-groomed beard. He never became an American citizen.

Mr. Williams made much of the importance of a formal way of life. He impressed upon his two sons from an early age the importance of literature to the cultivation of a truly worldly mind. "No man ever made a mark on the world of letters without reading," he admonished the boys, and this philosophy made a lasting impression upon young Willie. Every night after dinner, Mr. Williams gathered the family around him and read aloud from the Bible (especially favoring the prophet Isaiah), and from the poems and plays of his personal idol, William Shakespeare. He paid Willie one dollar per poem to memorize works from Francis Palgrave's *Golden Treasury of Songs and Lyrics*, thereby to enrich and strengthen himself.

Musical drama was Mr. Williams's great passion, and for many years, he directed local amateur productions of Gilbert and Sullivan operettas. He also encouraged Willie to take violin lessons. Mr. Williams's belief in the value of a sound education in all the arts was equaled only by his persistent emphasis upon lasting religious faith; he founded the Unitarian Society of Rutherford and served as Superintendent of the town Sunday School, which made it difficult for Willie and Ed to skip sessions. They attended faithfully each and every week.

William George Williams was a hard worker and responsible breadwinner. His sales job took him away from home for long periods of time on the road, in America and abroad, to Europe and South America. He returned with hair-raising tales to thrill and entertain his sons. He had a high sense of responsibility to his family, keeping a roof over their heads and food on the table.

But he was not the warmest of men. As a child, Willie feared his father more than loved him, a distant figure, who tried in his own fashion to be affectionate. He was the kind of father a son grows to understand better later on.

William Carlos Williams's mother was a woman as different from her husband as any wife could possibly be. Unlike William George, who was aloof and measured, she was a passionate, mystical woman with a hot temper and a sharp tongue. She hovered above her sons like a guardian angel, made of not quite the same stuff as mere mortals. Indeed, she often saw visions and heard voices from heavenly sources.

April, 1890: Willie and Ed were playing in the front yard of the family's second residence, at their farm in East Rutherford. A painted wooden fence of boards cut into scroll designs and tinted green and red, stretched above Willie's head, but he could peek through and see people passing by.

"Behind him," Williams remembered later, "his smaller brother, six years old or less, came following while the mother leaned upon the balustrade of the balcony that encircled the house and watched them. . . .

"There above . . . leaned nothing of America, but Puerto Rico, a foreign island in a tropical sea of earlier years—and Paris of later 1870s."

Raquel Helene Rose Hoheb Williams was born in Mayaguez, Puerto Rico, in 1847. She dreamed of studying fine arts in Paris, to live out a romantic idea of herself as an aristocrat. And so, at twenty-nine, she finally left Puerto Rico, with the blessing and financial support of her older brother and guide, the surgeon Carlos, who would become Willie's namesake.

A solitary painting by Raquel Helene survives from her heady days in Paris, "Portrait of a Niece in Mayaguez." It shows a talent that was never allowed to reach fulfillment. A girl's large, dark, and brooding eyes stare out from a face partly shadowed and partly touched by light. Her hair also has glints of light in it; but her mouth, pouting and full, is sad, and her large eyes, at first luminous, also turn melancholy the longer we look at them. The girl gazes vacantly into the distance, the future, dreaming.

After three short years in Paris, Raquel Helene retreated back to Puerto Plata, where brother Carlos introduced her to his friend the Englishman, William George Williams, a good man, who often came calling. A mere ten months after they met, the two were married. She withdrew into domestic life—a new home, in a new land, America. And, soon after, she had two new babies to care for.

Raquel Helene was a fish out of water in Rutherford. At least her husband, being British, spoke the language of America in his own formal way. But she was more comfortable with Spanish and French. She stayed close to the house and addressed her boys in foreign tongues.

She was a strange mixture of many streams, her son wrote of her, above all, "a romantic . . . discouragement and despair were violent, periodic factors in her life." Beneath her changing face was a tough core, which stood as an example for Willie. Her first, unbreakable rule was that he must *always* tell the truth. If Willie lied to his mother, and she found out, she did not hesitate to beat him across the backside with a chunk of firewood.

She was fond of telling him Spanish proverbs and stories. "The Spanish have a saying," she cried, shaking her finger in little Willie's face and raising her voice to frighten him, "*Malo, malo, malo, malo! Su te conocia en el falo!*" (Bad, bad, bad, bad—if they know you in your weakness.) No matter how defeated you may feel, don't let others see your faults, or it will simply make matters worse. Keep your chin up; present a hard look to the world.

Another one of her favorites was, *"Aguanta cachete y calla, porque si viene otra sera peor."* (A person who is punished, and slapped, says to himself, Be silent and stand for it, for if another blow comes, it will be worse.) She saw the world around her as an unsympathetic place, "Especially for people like *us*, Willie," Raquel Helene seemed to say, "people different than the crowd. We are so often the object of scorn, because they don't understand."

Willie was devoted to his parents and never tired of saying so throughout his life, expressing his love in poems and stories. While his father set goals for Willie and showed him the pure virtues of hard work, book learning, and upstanding behavior—pillars that were expected to support his middle-class way of life—his darkly mysterious mother was the first living example to Willie of a true artist.

His father and his mother were two opposite forces, and they would combine in Willie as time went on.

🙠

There were other Williamses at 131 West Passaic Avenue besides the parents and the two peas-in-a-pod-close, friendly, competitive brothers. Mr. Williams's mother, Grandma Wellcome, also lived with them. She taught Willie his first prayer, in a way the first poem he ever learned:

> *Gentle Jesus,*
> *Meek and mild,*
> *Look upon a simple child,*
> *Pity my simplicity.*

It was from his English grandmother that William Carlos Williams learned how to speak English, within the many-tongued atmosphere of his own home, where his parents usually conversed in Spanish.

Grandma Wellcome had two sons, William George Williams's younger half-brothers. They lived with the Williams family, too. Godwin, the older, seemed half mad to young Willie's innocent eyes. He was inclined to violent fits and insisted he was possessed by demons. He died in an asylum in Morris Plains just before World War I. Willie learned another kind of rhyme from Godwin and remembered it his whole life long:

> *Oh boys keep away*
> *From the girls I say*
> *And give them plenty of room*
> *For when you come to wed*
> *They'll bang you on the head*
> *With the bald-headed end*
>   *of a broom!*

Irving Wellcome, Willie's younger uncle, was a musical sort. He had a lovely baritone voice. Evenings after dinner he sang duets with Raquel Helene, or played the flute as she played piano. One time, he beat upon a toy drum for little Willie, who imitated him precisely on his own drum—"tum, tum, tum"—showing a precocious sense of rhythm and a keen ear. Irving was always the gentleman, favoring sports such as croquet and lawn tennis.

A constant flow of house guests from the tropical islands, old friends of Willie's parents from younger days, and of course visitors from England, too, dropped by for a weekend or a week, or more. The front door was always open.

ঙ্গ

No matter how hectic and crowded the scene at home became, Willie could always find his way over the back fence, to nature's beauty. He loved it more than life, and this simple delight never left him. It formed the roots for his dedication to poetry, his desire to recapture the feelings of a childhood spent with nature by his side.

From an early age, Willie exercised his eyes and ears. All his senses were alive. He loved the shift of seasons, anticipating with special delight the fading of winter into spring. He and Ed sometimes sneaked up to the attic, found their mother's long-abandoned tubes of paint and brushes, and dabbled with them, played with the bright colors. His mother encouraged in him a visual love of the world. She showed Willie how a simple inspiration, a smell, a glimpse, a few overheard words, could bring the past back: "A red rose in the garden," she singled out one day, "It seems to me that is the smell of the roses in that circle there in France—the first summer that I went." The past lived on inside her. She could not let it go, and her older son was the same way. Throughout his life, he valued every event, every memory, no matter how slight it might seem at the time.

What good did it do to understand, as Willie did, the "profound detail of the woods . . . the way the moss climbed about a tree's roots, what growing dogwood and ironwood looked like; the way rotten leaves will mat down in a hole —and their smell when turned over . . ."?

What was the practical use of knowing the difference, as Willie did, between a sparrow, a starling, a robin, a warbler, and a pigeon?

As Williams said years later, in *A Sketch for the Beginnings of an American Education*, it was first and foremost a boy's actual *experience*, even more than book-learning, which provided knowledge of life. And that knowledge, of seeing and doing things yourself—if a boy or girl were fortunate enough to know how to use it— would lead to freedom of imagination, letting the spirit run free. The best verse came out of constant contact with the world of experiences, doing things, meeting people, encountering nature. Poetry was not a fantasy world to William Carlos Williams. It was a way of expressing clearly what happened to a person when he felt something so deeply that he *had* to turn that feeling into written words.

❧

Under the green foliage, Willie hunted snakes, chipmunks, and squirrels. He stole apples from Mr. Kip's orchard, flew kites in the open meadow, and fished in fresh streams. These hours were sweet, and he spent many of them alone, imagining himself as a grown-up forester, tramping along undisturbed, listening to the comforting sound of dried leaves crunching underfoot and the occasional cry of an animal.

As a young boy, Willie hadn't a thought for *writing* poetry. He was too preoccupied with the sheer thrill he felt experiencing all the lovely things in this American town, this Rutherford, in Willie's childhood still part of the frontier.

Willie's beloved trees showed off their strength as the years turned. The trees were born, and died, and were always reborn again. When the winds came, the trees bent their backs to withstand the harsh weather's blasts. A young boy could admire endlessly, as he walked by every day, the bravery, the stamina, the fierce and stubborn beauty of the trees,

> *straining*
> *against the bitter horizontals of*
> *a north wind,—there below you*
> *how easily the long yellow notes*
> *of poplars flow upward in a descending*
> *scale, each note secure in its own*
> *posture—singularly woven.*

II

"I must make something of myself"

"Underneath it all, there was an enormous faith and solidity. Inside me I was like iron and with a love for the world that was like the ocean itself."

Every Sunday, in a routine Willie found reassuring, his father read the sermon after religious instruction at the Unitarian Church. Willie, dutifully seated in the congregation, sang hymns and felt cleansed, felt the "peace of God which passeth understanding" flow through him. For he had made a pact with himself. The spiritual glory he craved could be achieved only if he himself were perfect in every way. Willie Williams would strive for perfection in all areas of his life. He would tell the truth always, despite what others might say about it being an impossible standard to keep, now that the temptation of girls had been added to his world.

Truth was the keystone of Unitarian philosophy. To cherish it, now, as his lifelong standard! That decision once made, and renewed every Sunday, relief washing over him in waves of joy, Willie burst from the church's shadows and ran over the wide lawn, dashing away into the sunlight, his friends in hot pursuit. The idealistic spirit was so alive in Willie he could taste it.

In fact, running had become Willie's favorite way of moving through the day. That was all he wanted to do, and the other kids were hard-pressed to keep up with his frenzied activity. There was a sharply competitive side to all his driven movement. Willie hated to be beaten in anything: "I wasn't licked and never should be. No saint," he was the first to admit, though he aspired to a condition of saintliness, "but plenty of self-esteem." Willie's growing sense of inner values kept the others away. He outpaced many of his friends in his endless desire to be "alone, no ship, no person, no sound but the wind in my ears as I flew." He liked to break away from the pack, then rejoin it when he and he alone was completely ready.

From earliest youth, Willie had a sense of being different. It wasn't that he was a snob, or aloof; rather, he was a fierce individual who set tough goals for himself. In trying to achieve his goals, he forgot sometimes about other people and their strivings, the things they just might have had in common with him.

❧

In the fall of 1897, William George Williams went on a year-long business trip to South America. He decided to send his boys to school in Europe at the same time. Mother would accompany them. It would give Willie and Ed the precious chance (or so Mr. Williams firmly believed) to sample the rigorous standards of a continental education, and Mrs. Williams could revisit old friends from art school days in Paris. Although Raquel Helene never did in her lifetime go back to Puerto Rico, she did share this one important trip with her sons, the only time she went abroad as a married woman.

It was quite a leap for Willie. The fourteen-year-old boy gave up all the closeness and familiarity of small town life for the Chateau de Lancy in Geneva, Switzerland. The school had sixty-two boys from twelve different countries.

Willie found a way to make himself feel more at home during his first months on foreign soil. He collected wild-flowers and preserved them in a little book. Two of the flowers he found, the yellow primrose and the green asphodel, became subjects for poems many years later. And, looking back upon his Swiss school experience after half a century, Williams still recalled the vivid order of violets in the lush woods surrounding Chateau de Lancy, just as his mother remembered the roses in the courtyard of her artist days.

From Geneva, Willie, Ed, and Mrs. Williams traveled on to Paris, and six months at the renowned Lycée Condorcet, where the always-competitive Willie soon proved he could jump higher than any of the other boys in the school. They stayed with Raquel Helene's cousins, the Truflys. Monsieur Trufly was a cordial and eccentric fellow who took Willie and Ed under his wing, introducing them to the city's little-known highways and magical byways. Waving his walking stick gracefully in the air, he was their guide through churches and art galleries; took Willie and Ed to the Eiffel Tower; allowed them to sit with him and while away the hours at little cafés along the Left Bank.

It was all quite awe-inspiring, to move from the banks of the Passaic River to the banks of the Seine. Willie received an early taste of cosmopolitan life he never forgot. He returned to Paris several times as a young man. Its exotic atmosphere and stimulating people in all the arts always excited him, but he was ever anxious to come home to his familiar world, the comforting smallness of Rutherford.

Willie's Parisian walking excursions with his uncle were excellent training for the long treks he and Ed took with their father through the New Jersey countryside in the summers after they returned home. Mr. Williams's well-known belief in a sound mind included a healthy body; the threesome often covered more than twenty miles at a stretch. One time, they walked thirty-two miles, clear into Connecticut. "Put foot!" Pop Williams commanded to his boys, as they set off, strung out fifty feet apart along dusty country roads. Ed sketched pastoral scenes on postcards and mailed them back to his mother, while Willie, at sixteen lost in private reveries, stopped occasionally to collect birds' eggs or pick flowers along the roadside.

The seeds were sown for a young poet about to spring forth into bloom. "What makes one become a poet?" Williams wrote of those dreamy, moody days, "I suddenly realized as a boy—a man's position in the world is lonely."

Willie's childhood and teen years were awkward and passionate times, when he tested his strengths and tried to accept his limitations. In his heart of hearts, and with his mother's admonishings ringing in his ears, he tried equally hard to shrug off his shortcomings. He spent much of his time by himself, when he wasn't in school or at church services. Even in a group of kids, Willie felt that he *understood* solitude.

The painter finds colors; the poet finds words. Much like the spiritual surges he experienced in church, Willie had a one-to-one communion with nature. He had the raw materials for poetry in his mind. Soon he would be ready to give full expression to his newfound ideas. All he needed now was a gentle push in the right direction to get him started on a path which would involve him for his entire life.

That push came when Willie entered Horace Mann High in 1899. After two years of study abroad, he couldn't very well stay in the *local* school. Mr. Williams would not accept such a compromise in quality. No, his boys must attend the best place on the East Coast. What matter if it was an arduous journey every morning: walk to the Erie

Railroad station for the 7:00 train to the Hudson River ferry; then, a tossing, spray-dampened ride across the river —Willie's favorite position was at the prow—then, once at Chambers Street on the other side, walk up to the Ninth Avenue Elevated subway, take that to 116th Street. The boys followed the same path every night back home, rain or shine.

At Horace Mann, Willie found out what it meant to work. Determined, he began the year with a roster of courses emphasizing science, chemistry, physics, and mathematics. Under the tutelage of his English teacher, "Uncle Billy" Abbott, Willie actually *looked* at a poem for the first time. He felt the excitement of being in the presence of great books. It was not his first encounter with poetry, by any means. But at Horace Mann, he learned about literature in a new way, because he was being asked to form his very own opinions about what he read. He approached poetry in a more intellectual way than at home, in the past.

Samuel Taylor Coleridge's (1772–1834) "Rime of the Ancient Mariner," with its lyrical, narrative journey, impressed Willie. Coleridge was also a critic, who saw the imagination as a "magical power," the primary force behind all human perception, connected to the divine source of power coming from God; thus did poets create.

According to Coleridge's theory, the imagination revealed itself in poets who had the ability to put together "a more than usual state of emotion, with more than usual order." That description suited the passionate and equally shy Willie Williams quite well.

Mr. Abbott also introduced the boys to the works of John Milton (1608–1674). "L'Allegro" and "Il Penseroso" were two companion poems about "the happy man" and "the thoughtful man." Willie appreciated these qualities, as they reflected the opposite sides of his own nature.

But Willie's favorite poet of all was John Keats (1795–1821). Like the other English Romantic poets of his day— Shelley, Byron, Wordsworth—who saw poetry as "the

spontaneous overflow of powerful feelings," Keats believed
the poet should be involved with life on a deeper level than
most people. He said, "The excellence of every art is its
intensity."

In Keats's "Ode on a Grecian Urn," Willie found the
famous lines which sounded so well in tune with his Unitarian background:

> *"Beauty is truth, truth beauty,"—that is all*
> *Ye know on earth, and all ye need to know.*

It is fortunate that English class satisfied Willie's
spiritual needs, because he was not the most accomplished
student at Horace Mann. His report card showed many
C's and D's. Perhaps his head was too often in the clouds
instead of burrowed between the pages of a book. Perhaps
the long commute to school or his desire to become a track
star left him exhausted. That took hours of practice every
day. While brother Ed went out for team sports, baseball
especially, Willie preferred to pound the cinders alone,
mainly in competition with himself.

His mathematics teacher, Mr. Bickford, showed remarkable insight into young Willie's truer intentions:
"You'll never be a mathematician, Williams," he told the
boy after one particularly disastrous exam, "but you show
an understanding of the process! And I'm going to pass
you!"

"An understanding of the process." Yes, even if he
did not get the answers right, Willie had an intuitive grasp
of how ideas came to be. He could pick his way down a
problem's path, through thickets, toward the light—but
once he entered the clearing, he became confused by what
he saw there.

Willie struggled to master the three hundred-yard run.
During a race in his third year at Horace Mann, he thought

he was nearing the end of the course, when someone called out from the sidelines that there was still one more lap to go. Willie pushed on—and collapsed. The family doctor diagnosed the problem as adolescent heart strain. Whatever the cause, Willie was confined to bed for several weeks. It was the end of his track career.

But out of a period of disillusionment and depression following his illness, Willie's first poem was born. Thirteen wonderful words came to him in a rush:

> *A black, black cloud*
> *flew over the sun*
> *driven by fierce flying*
> *rain.*

"How could clouds be driven by rain?" he asked himself, thinking the poem "stupid" upon reflection. Casting aside logic, and the self-doubt that comes with the moment when any composition is finished, there it was, for the first time, *an original poem*, made up of air, fire, and water—and feeling.

One after another, Willie's secret notebooks, in the past filled with pressed flowers, now thickened with verses. Now that he had written a poem, poetry became a permanent part of his experience.

·~§

He still had to face an immediate and practical problem. It was the spring of his final year at Horace Mann. What should his next move be? The fight between the contradictory sides of Willie's personality had just begun. "Words offered themselves and I jumped at them," he declared bravely; that was simple enough to accept. He was willingly caught in the web of language.

He was afraid, too, for "poetry was a dangerous subject for a boy to fool with . . . I was caught up by the fascination of it," Willie confessed, "and forgot the warning

—for my father warned me to give poetry a wide berth."
Those quiet, thoughtful evenings reading Shakespeare by
lamplight in the Williams household were meant to develop the boy's cultured side. All young people were expected to be able to recite verse from memory. But to
pursue poetry as a livelihood? To *be* a poet? Who ever
heard of such a thing?

The pressures of his upbringing, however, were not
enough to deter young Willie Williams. He saw pleasure
in being able to tell people off through his writing; and
beyond that lay the tantalizing ideal of the writer's freedom. He had already tasted a little bit of it, and it was
pleasant to imagine that no one would ever tell him what
to write. He would say what he wanted, exactly how he
wanted, for whatever reason at whatever time the spirit
seized him. He would try to make something beautiful and
true out of his emotions that other people could understand and respect. Poetry would not simply be entertain-
ment for Willie. He was far too serious in his intentions.

On the other hand, turning the problem around in his
feverish brain yet again, he knew that he "didn't intend to
die for art, nor to be bedbug food for it, nor to ask anyone
for help." Willie showed his down-to-earth, practical side.
He knew full well that no poet lived entirely off the fruits
of his imagination alone, no matter how inspired he was.
The most powerful images in the world might well move
readers to tears of joy or rage, but they would not pay the
rent or the grocery bills.

Willie was not going to give in to the fate of a starv-
ing poet in his garret, subsisting on crumbs. Like his father,
he, too, would work, in the world and of it. He would live
first in order to free himself to write.

&

William Carlos Williams had the work ethic deeply in-
grained. The living example of his father as a constant pro-
vider stood before him. And he had his mother's legacy:

his middle name. Raquel Helene's father died when she was eight years old, and several older siblings had also died between her, and elder brother Carlos, ten years her senior. Carlos had raised Raquel Helene. He was a doctor. She greatly admired him. This ancestral influence may have been secretly working upon Willie. He had to live up to his name, thereby fulfilling his mother's unspoken hope.

It was decided. He would go to medical school. He certainly possessed the ingredients necessary to become a good physician: discipline, intellectual stamina (if not yet the ability), innate curiosity, and sensitivity. Besides, had not Willie's poetic idol, John Keats, studied surgery in London in his early twenties and became qualified to practice medicine?

This momentous double decision, partly Willie's and partly his parents', to be sure, began a pattern that continued through his life. His search for the materials with which to make his poems always had to take place in the real world, the world of people, things, and events. The practice of medicine kept him squarely in that realm. Then, in order to write, he had temporarily to leave day-to-day contact with people, and enter the inner world of his imagination where, in cherished solitude, the poem was put together—sometimes quickly, more often with as much painstaking care as he took in the delivery of a new baby.

In the fall of 1902, Willie Williams, just nineteen years old, entered the University of Pennsylvania School of Medicine in Philadelphia. He was the second youngest in a class of one hundred and twenty students.

III

"By the road to the contagious hospital"

William Carlos Williams was immediately homesick. Out from under the protective wing of his family for the first time, his loneliness was made more intense because—qualified through a special examination to enter medical school directly from high school—he was not enrolled as an undergraduate at Penn. He missed out on many activities of college life.

Willie remained close to his rooms that first term. Embryology, histology, anatomy, and neurology courses kept him at his books. His vow of perfection was still foremost in his mind. Now, he added to his other self-imposed standards a scientist's humility and caution. Willie was the one in the classroom who more often than not kept silence, let others commit themselves to a position. He took it all in, preferred to absorb information rather than show off what he knew. He struck a pose of reflection and formality that sometimes went to extremes when he signed the earliest letters home to his own mother, "Willie C. Williams."

Unlike almost all his acquaintances, Willie did not join a fraternity, which would have automatically put him in with a ready-made circle of young men, instant friends. And he declined to go out drinking with the crowd on weekends to neighborhood taverns. Every Sunday morning, as he had done while growing up in Rutherford, he attended services at the First Unitarian Church of Philadelphia.

A good boy, Willie reported dutifully to his parents in almost daily letters home. Toward Christmas of his first year at Penn, he forced himself to attend a dance: "I was introduced to about fifteen young ladies," he confessed to his mother on December 9, 1902. "My only regret is that now I have started I may be invited to more dances and it is either a case of refusing or finding a gold mine somewhere. I don't like these kinds of dances much, because they are too formal. The people I meet are too sporty for me."

Willie felt self-conscious about going out on the town because he did not have much money. He knew his father had worked hard to send him and brother Ed to the finest schools. Ed was now at M.I.T. studying architecture and that, too, was expensive. Willie was anxious to grow up and become a wage-earning citizen who could take care of himself.

Lacking the cash to buy a ticket, Willie sneaked into the Botanical Gardens to see the play, *As You Like It*, by his beloved Shakespeare. His father would certainly have approved of the fact that he saw the play, but not of the way in which he got in!

Willie tried out for the prestigious Mask and Wig Club, Penn's dramatic society. As a boy, he had performed in his father's production of Gilbert and Sullivan's *The Mikado*, and so he sang "Tit Willow" for the audition; then went on to play the role of Polonius, the wise old courtier, in a production of *Hamlet*. That was sure to make his parents proud. He harbored fantasies of writing his own plays, becoming a famous dramatist some day. Perhaps he should drop medicine altogether. His simple, two-sided decision no longer seemed so simple.

Drama was not enough. A young man had to keep his body in shape. Track was out, of course, due to the high school accident. He joined the Varsity fencing team instead, an appropriately gentlemanly sport for the slight, agile Willie, who stood five feet nine and weighed one hundred and thirty-five pounds.

Drama and sports were still not enough. Willie poured his private, poetic thoughts night after night into secret notebooks, confiding to himself, writing down desires and fears which never made their way into letters home, but had to be expressed somewhere, somehow by this frustrated young man, whose creative impulses pushed him in directions contrary to the way of medicine.

Dancing, drama, fencing, studying, some painting, and poetry still did not satisfy his energies. He scratched out tunes on his trusty fiddle. As for girls? Coming from an all-boys' school, Willie was too frightened, too full of yearning to do anything about girls for the time being except notice them, on all sides.

⋘

Mr. and Mrs. Williams soon detected a change in their older son. When he came home for the holidays, it seemed as if all the family did was spend their time around the dinner table in prolonged, bitter arguments. William George Williams was a tough adversary who dug in and held his ground, especially when provoked. But oh, how Willie wanted above all else to please his parents! Couldn't they see the struggle waging within him? He wanted to be respectable and keep his mind on medical studies. But that infernal, nagging, dangerous poetry kept distracting him into reading books he was not supposed to read and writing down ideas he was not supposed to have.

"I have always tried to do all that you and Papa wished me to do," Willie wrote his mother, "and many times I have done things against my own feelings because you wanted me to . . . I try to do right," he continued urgently, "and then I am blamed for doing wrong and it really is hard to be happy then."

What *was* the right thing? Hadn't he himself decided not to choose *between* medicine and writing, but to carry on steadfastly with both? Did he have the strength to maintain the double burden, or was he unrealistic? Should he devote himself to making others happy, achieving peace of mind; or should he stick even closer to self-discipline? When he came back alone to his room in the dorm on a Friday evening, facing the weekend without companionship, Willie lost himself in his work. There was always one more notebook to fill. His mind burned with poetry. In the end, there were twenty-eight notebooks in a row above his bed, where he contemplated them every day, and wondered about his future as a writer.

❧

Willie Williams was the kind of person who didn't have time to waste on frivolous socializing with people who had nothing to contribute. All he needed was patience, until he met someone else who saw at once that Willie, too, was cut from different cloth.

"Well, if you're interested in writing," a sophomore in Willie's dorm, Morrison Robb Van Cleve, mentioned to him one day during fall term, 1902, "there's a man in our class—he's a crazy guy—but I think you two would get along marvelously together. I'll bring him around."

The other fledgling writer was Ezra Loomis Pound, Willie's first college friend, and "the livest, most intelligent, and unexplainable thing he'd ever seen." Ezra was two years younger than Willie. A sophomore at the University, he majored in literature. He was born in Hailey, Idaho, and raised from the age of two in Wyncote, a suburb of Philadelphia, where his family had a large and comfortable home. Ezra enrolled at Penn, as he put it, "to

study what I thought important." He was a proud, arrogant young man, who held his head of wavy blond hair
high and sported a walking stick, a cloak, and a flowing
cravat.

The quality of his life before and after meeting Ezra,
Williams recalled years later, "was like B.C. and A.D."
Here, in the flesh, for the first time, was a contemporary, a
fellow poet who was not afraid to admit it; and whose passion for literature and the arts was undeniable.

Ezra was interested only in building audiences for his
own poetry. Willie took one of his thick, stiff-covered
notebooks, impressively bound in marbleized paper, down
from the shelf above his bed and read some quick, spontaneous poems to his newfound colleague. Ezra was not
impressed. But when he reciprocated, and read his work
to Willie, Ezra revealed the most annoying affectation,
letting his voice die down at the end of each line. How was
Willie supposed to respond to the poems, if he could not
hear them?

And Ezra had some theories about book learning that
shook Willie's carefully wrought standards: You didn't
have to read *all* the books you talked about, just be able
to say something witty about them when necessary. He
was, indeed, a brilliant talker who tended to dominate
most conversations.

◄§

Ezra Pound, being from the Philadelphia area, invited
Willie out to his home for meals many times, where they
had long, involved discussions about books, which Willie,
weighed down with medical training, had little time to
study. Literature was at the center of Ezra's life and always
would be; Willie still agonized over just what role it should
play in his future.

Homer Loomis Pound, Ezra's father, was a gold and
silver assayer in the United States Mint in Philadelphia.

Hearty, informal, with a very kind, Old-World manner, he was not too pleased with the figure this poetic son of his cut around the University. Isabel, his mother, was charming, shy, well bred. Their house in Wyncote became Willie's home away from home.

Most of the other students thought Ezra was eccentric, but Willie caught on to his brilliant and complex friend very quickly: "Not one person in a thousand likes him, and a great many detest him, and why? Because he is so darned full of conceits and affectations." Willie was attracted to Ezra because of his sharp mind, but also because he sensed a paradox in his personality, the way he "delights himself in making himself just exactly what he is not—a laughing boor." Willie took pleasure in seeking out the Ezra Pound beneath the mask; running true beneath the artificial mood was sincerity beyond question, and Willie's faith in this important quality gained him Ezra's friendship, a difficult prize, hard-won and hard-kept.

They used to argue, as they would their whole lives. Willie said "bread" and Ezra shot back, "caviar." The humble doctor-in-training, preparing himself for a life among the common people, challenged the scholarly, snobbish lad preparing himself for a life of culture.

Yes, Willie *liked* Ezra. But he didn't want to *be like* him.

&

"Writing has parts precisely as the human body has also," Willie observed at the beginning of his medical education, "If a man is to know it, it behooves him to become familiar with those parts."

Unfortunately, virtually none of Willie's student efforts at poetry survive. He did, however, talk often in later years about the important influence Walt Whitman's poetry had upon him in those early days of writing. Whitman was the first American poet to attract Willie's attention, because of his passion: "When I was inclined to write poems," Williams recalled, "I was very definitely an American kid," as American, no doubt, as the Good Grey Poet himself.

Walt Whitman (1819–1892) was a journeyman printer, a schoolteacher, and a journalist in and around the New York City area where he grew up. His most famous work, the collection *Leaves of Grass*, was published in 1855, and attracted the attention of Ralph Waldo Emerson, who heralded the young poet at the beginning of what he predicted would be a great career. His poems, the first in America to break from the traditional verse forms of English poetry, glorified self-discovery and praised a sensual life.

Willie was particularly moved when he read Whitman's long poem, "Song of Myself." The opening lines caught his eye, because they touched upon the same inner search for awareness that Willie took so seriously:

I celebrate myself, and sing myself,
And what I assume you shall assume,
For every atom belonging to me as good belongs to you.

Whitman drew Willie into his spell. Indeed, until a person thought well of *himself*, how could he go forth to encounter the rest of the world? Later in the poem, Whitman hinted at the mystery of the soul:

There is that in me—I do not know what it is—
but I know it is in me.

When Willie read Whitman's poetry, he understood that part of the task of becoming a poet was the ability to live with these mysteries.

Willie's notebooks contained free thoughts and passionate, private insights in the style of Whitman. Only Ezra Pound was trusted enough to hear them.

He was also writing sonnets, imitating his other idol, John Keats. These formal, elegant, and romantic verses were included in letters to confidant-brother Ed and composed for the ears of certain special young ladies.

For several years, Willie was also at work on a long, four-part poem modeled after Keats's "Endymion." A prince in Willie's poem nearly dies in a family tragedy, only to be saved by the faithful nurse who has raised him since infancy. Alas, the hero, finding himself in an unfamiliar forest, aimlessly wanders to and fro, and spends most of the poem trying to find his way back to home ground.

Early in his fourth year at Penn, Willie—anxious to show his epic poem to someone he respected—journeyed to Boston to visit the distinguished M.I.T. professor, Arlo Bates. Brother Ed convinced Willie this was the man to see. In the back of his mind the question still burned, with a mere seven months left to medical school: *Should he quit, and follow the creative life exclusively, or should he, must he, go on with medicine?* The even-tempered resolution with which he began medical studies now wavered dangerously.

Dr. Bates flipped through the numerous pages of Willie's manuscript, with its lines and lines of copperplate script in iambic pentameter, then peered up over his half-glasses at the nervous young man standing before him in the shadowy study. "You have done some creditable imitations of Keats's work. No bad," he intoned, then paused, while Willie's heart beat quickly and he swallowed a few times. Dr. Bates continued, choosing his words carefully, "Perhaps in twenty years, yes, in perhaps twenty years, you may succeed in attracting some attention to yourself." Another long pause: "In the meantime, go on with your medical studies."

Despite the bleak sound of that prophecy, Willie breathed more easily. It was an important lesson. It would take time and labor to develop a voice that was his very

own, and not merely a skillful reproduction of a poet he
admired. Would those years be worth it, in the end? Nobody could answer that question for Willie Williams.

❧

There was something attractive about the carefully dressed,
shy young man across the dinner table from Willie at the
boarding house on Locust Street where he took his meals;
something enigmatic about that drawn face, those piercing
dark eyes, the sleek black hair. The young man had a way
of tilting his head down and away when he answered a
question. But he was well-spoken, and when the discussion
turned to painting—the thing he loved most to do in the
whole world—the stranger leaped to life.

His name was Charles Demuth. He was studying art
at Drexel University when Willie met him during late
fall term, 1903. They became instant friends; each one
was interested in what the other was up to. Willie
Williams was still a "Sunday painter," paying frequent
visits to the studio of an older artist named John Wilson,
who set up an easel for him, with paints and brushes, and
urged Willie to try his hand. And when paints frustrated
him, Charlie Demuth, in his turn, toyed with the idea of
becoming a writer some day.

Charlie was born in 1883, the same year as Willie.
He grew up in Lancaster, Pennsylvania. In those days, it
was a town much like Rutherford, surrounded by farm-
land, a quiet place with austere, regular rows of brownstone buildings. When Willie met him, Charlie was concentrating upon delicate watercolors of plants and flowers.
Because of his fragile condition—Charlie was lame from a
hip injury sustained when he was four years old; and he
later discovered he suffered from diabetes, the disease
which ultimately killed him at the age of fifty-two—he
spent long periods of time at home. His mother cultivated
what was said to be the finest garden in Lancaster, a little
sanctuary criss-crossed by red brick paths, set far back from

the street. Charlie sat there in seclusion for hours sketching the lovely blooms. In later years, he established a studio on the second floor overlooking the garden. The house, 118 East King Street, was his retreat from the world.

Charlie Demuth and Willie Williams took long, slow walks after dinner, down Philadelphia's narrow streets. The two came to realize just how much they had in common, including a growing desire to write about, or paint, what was closest to hand. They agreed that was the most important goal for any artist: to focus upon what he knew or could imagine best.

In 1904, Charlie made a definite decision to pursue a full-fledged painting career, transferring most of his studies to the prestigious Pennsylvania Academy of Fine Arts. Unlike Willie, he came from a background of independent means. His family supported his work, and he was able to travel often, to New York City and to Europe. But in his subject matter, Charlie Demuth remained in touch with familiar flowers in light and shadow, arching gracefully out of their pots. He portrayed the rapidly changing landscape around his hometown, the factories and grain elevators and warehouses springing up on all sides.

Charlie and Willie grew together into their respective crafts. "Carlos, Carlos," he wrote to his friend in September, 1907, just before leaving on a trip abroad, "I have always felt that it would happen to you some day—that you would simply *have* to write . . . To feel the joy of creating for a single moment seems to repay one for a year's work. . . ." It helped to have a few people in his life who truly understood Willie selflessly, as Charlie did. Yes, it was painful to wait for a poem to emerge. And the painter possessed such deep insights and sensitivity for one so young: "When you feel like giving it all up," Charlie went on sympathetically, "then you think: what *would* become of me if I *really* were made to give it up forever?" Charlie Demuth helped Willie confront these hard questions, helped him to see his way more clearly through troubling times of confusion and self-doubt.

Between Charlie's hectic trips to the boulevards of Paris and the night life of New York City, the peace and safety of his mother's home—and, finally, sadly, extended stays for treatment of diabetes at a sanatorium in Morristown, New Jersey—he kept in close touch with his old and dear friend "Carlos."

Willie always had an understanding of painting. He had grown up in an artistic household. He spoke the language of art, tried to accomplish the same goals with words that Charles Demuth and other painter friends later on were attempting within their chosen medium: to capture the truth as he saw it, and translate it into a form of expression purely his own. There really wasn't that much new to be said, by anyone; it was all in the *way* you said something.

Willie continued to flirt with painting until 1914, when it became clear that the demands of his busy medical practice prevented him from setting up an easel and mixing paints. All that preparation took too long; the quick, spontaneous way he jotted down notes was more suited to Willie's frantic lifestyle.

ܐܒ

After nearly three years at Penn, Willie was beginning to despair of ever meeting any girls who shared his passion for the arts and for nature; girls who appreciated his sensitive side, who didn't care whether or not he was a good dancer.

On a fine afternoon in April, 1905, friend Ezra, home for spring break from Hamilton College, where he was continuing his studies in Romance languages and literature, invited Willie out to the house at Wyncote for a party. Of the several young women there, one caught Willie's eye: Hilda Doolittle, a student of Greek and classical literature at nearby Bryn Mawr College. "She is tall," he wrote excitedly to Ed, "about as tall as I am, young, about eighteen, and, well, not round and willowy, but rather bony, no that doesn't express it, just a little clumsy and all to the mustard."

More important, Hilda had an air of mystery about her, hints of hidden strength and attractiveness Willie so much admired: "She's a girl that's full of fun," he told Ed, "bright, but never telling you all she knows, doesn't care if her hair is a little mussed, and wears good solid shoes. She is frank and loves music and flowers and I got along with her pretty well."

The following weekend, Willie found himself taken in for dinner at the Doolittles' cozy country home in Upper Darby. Hilda, with five brothers, was the only daughter and favorite child of the eminent Charles Doolittle, Professor of Mathematics and Astronomy at the University of Pennsylvania. Her mother, Helen, was a musician and artist.

Professor Doolittle, tall and stooped, with his flowing white beard, dominated the family scene. He sat at the head of the table, concentrating upon his meal, until an important idea struck him. Mrs. Doolittle had to be constantly ready for such momentous occasions. He cleared his throat. "Your father is about to speak!" Mrs. Doolittle announced. All immediately fell silent. Then, "his eyes fixed on nothing nearer than the moon," the professor pronounced what he had to say; after which, life could go on as before.

He was a distant figure, who expected his children to be seen and not heard. He spent most nights in the observatory, studying the cosmos. On exceptionally cold winter nights, or so the story went, after having been at his work until dawn, his whiskers became frozen to the telescope eyepiece. His wife was standing by to thaw them out with a kettle of boiling water.

Hilda Doolittle had a good dosage of her father's eccentric nature in her. She was a flighty, coltish girl, who always seemed to be slipping away—at least from Willie. Despite her breathlessness, he was infatuated with her.

After dinner at the Doolittles, the boys and girls took an informal walk through the surrounding countryside. In those days, "informal" meant that the girls wore short skirts, only to their ankles, and sweaters, and no hats; and most of the boys left their hats behind, too.

They set out as a group. The fresh air and sunshine brightened their cheeks. Hilda, her hair blowing this way and that in the breeze, led the way. She knew exactly where all the finest flower beds were, the violets, hepaticas, and deep-blue grape hyacinths. Soon enough, Hilda and Willie were alone, in a spring meadow, far from their rowdy companions. They strolled deeper into the woods and spent several hours talking of only the finest things, Shakespeare (his favorite writer and hers), the wonders of nature, books of all kinds. They walked and walked, until before they knew it, the sun began to set and they had to turn back home.

By the time he finally staggered to his dorm past midnight, Willie was in heaven, bewitched by Hilda's "loose-limbed beauty." When he was with her, he wrote, his "feet always seemed to be sticking to the ground, while she would be walking on the tips of the grass stems." She called him "Billy," or, sometimes playfully, "William Squared."

Another day, during another secret walk, she told him that, to help herself loosen up and get started writing poems, she splattered ink on her dress.

One afternoon, they were caught in a sudden rainstorm. Willie sought shelter under a tree, but free-spirited Hilda stood in the middle of the field, spread out her arms, tilted her head back, and called out to the heavens, "Come, beautiful rain! Beautiful rain, welcome!"

She was Willie's first muse. He composed an acrostic for her, a sonnet, in which the first word of each line and each word following began with the letters of her name:

Hark, Hilda! heptachorian hymns
Invoke the year's initial ides
Like liquid lutes' low languishings.
Dim dawn defeated dusk derides.
Awake, for at Aurora's advent angel anthemings
arise!

Willie Williams was not Hilda's only admirer.

Ezra Pound had been her friend since they first met at a Halloween party in 1901, when she was a mere fifteen, and he was sixteen. During undergraduate days, the friendship grew far more serious than dressing up in playful costumes. One of Hilda's brothers built a platform high in the huge maple tree in the family garden, so high it could not be seen from the ground; so secret that when you were concealed in it, you could not even see the house.

Hilda and Ezra spent many spring and summer afternoons up there, when they weren't hiding in his family's apple orchard, reading poetry to each other. As he did for his friend Willie, Ezra bought Hilda books to study and told her which authors she should profitably read: Balzac, Ibsen, Shaw, Whistler, William Morris. He called her his "Dryad," a wood-nymph whose life was bound up with her tree. She called him her pesky "Gadfly."

Like Willie, Hilda did not care if the school girls thought Ezra was crazy. She liked the fact that he was not like the others. He was a generous and loving teacher.

Once a sultry afternoon had come to an end. It was time for them to part, Ezra to catch the last trolley, then a train to Wyncote. "There is another trolley in a half hour," Hilda said, preparing to slide out of the secret crow's nest. "No, Dryad," the ardent Ezra replied, and then, Hilda remembered, "He snatches me back. We sway with the wind. There is no wind. We sway with the stars. They are not far. We slide, slip, fly down through the branches, leap together to the ground. 'No,' I say, breaking from his arms. 'No,' drawing back from his kisses."

Like Willie, Ezra, too, wrote poems for the beloved Hilda. But he went further. He bound twenty-five verses into a little book he made himself, covered in vellum,

> *a little book . . .*
> *Quaint bound, as 'twere in parchment very old*
> *That all my dearest words of her should hold*

Ezra wrote of her as

> *Child of the grass . . .*
> *Thou that art sweeter than all orchards' breath*
> *And clearer than the sun gleam after rain . . .*
> *a lady tall and fair to see*
> *She swayeth as a poplar tree*
> *When the wind bloweth merrily*

Another warm, fateful day, Professor Doolittle walked in on Hilda and Ezra embracing in his favorite armchair. "Mr. Pound," he pronounced, as the blushing couple leaped up, "I will not forbid you the house, but I will ask you not to come so often."

As far as Hilda's parents could tell, Ezra, a poet, had no respectable job or intentions. He was a bad influence, a loner, nothing better than a nomad.

Ezra gave Hilda a ring; his mother gave her a pearl pendant. But their brief, on-again, off-again, always-unofficial engagements over six years were bound to fail.

~§

Willie repeated over and over that he absolutely, positively was *not* in love with Hilda; he knew she was Ezra's rightful girlfriend and knew it well. Willie told Ezra his intentions were no more than friendly; Hilda was just a kindred spirit, a girl he could talk to about anything at all. But into his fourth and final year at Penn, and unknown to Ezra, Willie often made the trip out to Upper Darby to see her. "I call her Hilda now," he boasted gleefully to Ed; and in May, 1906, as graduation neared, he finally confessed to his younger brother that "I'm dead in love with that girl. She isn't good looking and she isn't graceful, she isn't a beautiful dresser and cannot play any music, but by Gee! she is a fine girl and she can have me alright."

Hilda knew she could have Willie. But she didn't want him quite that way. He was forced to go to the senior graduation dance with another girl. Hilda longed for Ezra. Her love was frustrated by her family's opposition especially her father's, for she was the apple of his eye. Meanwhile, Ezra the wanderer slipped away. After receiving his M.A., he left for Spain in June, 1906, and did not return for a year. In 1911, Hilda followed him to London, where he helped sponsor her first publication in a magazine as the poet "H.D., Imagiste." Finally, they both married other people: Ezra found Dorothy Shakespear; Hilda moved in with the English writer, Richard Aldington.

William Carlos Williams learned much in his tumultuous four years at Penn. His friends showed him where his heart was and thankfully distracted him from medical studies, widening his world considerably. He discovered just how romantic he really was, beyond poetry, and how dedicated he was to people he cared about.

But Willie also learned he was fated to live with a constant inner battle. He was going to have to face the inevitable struggle driving the artist in him forward. He was going to have to live and experience what seemed on the surface to be an ordinary enough life, working at medicine every day so that he could carve out time and find material for his craft of verse. Willie understood that it was his duty to learn medicine because he needed to write poetry. It was his responsibility to learn how to help others so he could then help himself.

"Remember," he told Ed, "you are going to live forever and that's no damned fool poetic figure, it's got to be true for you to be happy." Thinking of his poetry, and of the poet's search for truth, Willie continued, "We must therefore do things that will last forever."

He did not have much time to reflect upon these realizations after graduation from Penn in June, 1906.

IV

"*The young doctor is dancing with happiness*"

Just one week out of medical school, William Carlos Williams moved to the big city, New York, to begin work as an intern—fourteen-hour days, sometimes longer, during the hot summer—on the wards of the French Hospital, at Thirty-fourth Street between Ninth and Tenth Avenues.

It was a new, tougher life in constant contact with the city's poor people, waterfront workers, fishermen, sailors, drunks off the street, construction men from the new Pennsylvania Station site further east; all-night vigils in the emergency room where Williams sewed up stab wounds, pumped stomachs, and mended skulls fractured in Saturday night brawls.

He wanted the challenge and he wanted the change. It appealed to his fascination with newness of any kind. He liked his independence, as long as it wasn't too extreme. He could, and did, go home weekends to Rutherford to see childhood friends and gain the approval of his family.

The life of a surgeon was not for Williams. He liked face-to-face contact, the chance to talk through what ailed a person, to arrive at a diagnosis, probing, questioning, pursuing any mystery that came his way. His would be a general practice, more suited to his mercurial personality.

At French Hospital, Williams's intense, lonely routine became even more rigorous than it had been at Penn. The textbooks were left behind; in their stead were sick people, demanding attention at all hours. Williams was up at seven each morning, eating breakfast with the other house staff by seven-thirty. Then, from eight to ten, he went on morning rounds, and was expected to see every patient in the hospital. His job was to determine their recuperation progress, make entries on their charts, recommend medication or changes in treatment if necessary, and then be ready to go over each case with the visiting senior physician from ten in the morning until one in the afternoon. The rest of the day was spent visiting newly admitted patients. After an early dinner, Williams was back on rounds again, which usually took him to nine, when he retired to his little room to rest or write.

Williams was still at work on his all-important poetry, discovering how much harder it was than he had thought to keep at it with a real-life job to do; and at the same time, for that very reason, how much more it meant to him to continue with the poems. He fought the despair that came over him late at night in his hospital room, the same feeling he used to have in his dorm at Penn: Did anyone besides himself *really* care what he was writing? What difference could yet another poem make to anyone? Restlessly and nervously, Williams wrote, because he had to be active, always at work. He was dedicated to the higher goal of hard work beyond its difficulties, to make, like Keats, a thing of beauty. He was a frenetic young man in hurried search of answers to uncertain questions.

But he was *not* writing poems about the sick and dying, odes to broken bones, sonnets in praise of a newborn babe in its mother's arms. Williams had not yet made the connection between poetry and actual experience. He had not yet discovered that the whole universe was suitable for the poem. He still wrote "pure," romantic poetry in sonnet form; poetry higher than, apart from, bloody and painful life on the hospital wards.

He told Ed, "To do what I mean to do and to be what I must be in order to satisfy my own self, I must discipline my affections, and until a first opportunity affords, must like no one in particular except you, Ed, and my nearest family . . . I have a weakness where passion is concerned." Williams risked no serious involvement with the many nurses who worked side by side with him every day, several of whom were pressing for marriage. He did not want to become overly concerned about his patients, either, but it was hard not to feel for them.

After nearly two years at French, from July, 1906, to May, 1908, Williams continued his training, again, with only a one-week break. He transferred to Nursery and Child's Hospital, further uptown at Sixty-first Street and Tenth Avenue, where he specialized in children's diseases, obstetrics, and family practice.

It was another dangerous neighborhood; but Williams now had less to do with victims of shootings and muggings than with impoverished women in final months and weeks of pregnancy, many of them without husbands, who lived on the hospital wards until they bore their children, then often gave the babies up to the state for care.

Williams took to pediatric work immediately, became devoted to the foundling infants, knew them all by name— or invented names for them—and in the course of his stay at the hospital delivered more than three hundred babies.

Like the doctor, the poet developed his senses above those of most people, so he could see, feel, and touch what other men took for granted, as signs of illness, signs of life within himself or within a woman coming to term. Like the doctor, the poet needed to develop a skill at active waiting; he had to know when to act and when to wait, and to move quickly when the right moment arrived—for labor, with babies and with poems, was long, and delivery speedy. The struggle to bring forth life could take many, many hours, sometimes days—but the moment of truth, for newborns and new poems alike, was brief.

Like the doctor, the poet *cared*, despite his grumblings and complaints; and he still had to dig deeply and find enough caring left over after a day delivering babies—to write. Williams sometimes remarked that at last, at the end of the day, he was so tired that finally he could compose a poem. He pushed himself close to the edge of fatigue. Like the doctor, the poet learned to live with constant tiredness. Then, the words came.

ک

"One thing that has helped me immeasurably," Williams wrote to Ed, "is the idea that I have that some day I can show the world something more beautiful than it has ever seen before."

He was truly an idealistic poet, and a defiant one. What was the best way, he asked himself, to show the world how he had been spending all those long hours in his rooms? By putting a book of poems together. He had been acting occasionally in an amateur dramatics group in Rutherford; and his first play, *Betty Putnam*, was produced early in 1909 at the local tennis club. He even flirted occasionally with the idea of becoming a playwright full time. But the *poems* still cried out for release.

Williams was twenty-five years old. His career in medicine was underway. It was time to create an audience for his work, however small. After all, what good is a poem, if it hides in a desk drawer?

The question became, how to bring out such a book? Williams had not made any connections in the publishing world. That happened later, and even then with decidedly mixed results. He had not yet sent out any of his poems to literary magazines. Out of fear and hesitation, his readership had been confined thus far to friends and family.

It was not uncommon, in Williams's day, for a would-be author to go directly to a printer with his work, then sell the finished book directly to stores. Self-publishing had a proud, noble tradition. Many poets before William Carlos Williams had done it, often printing the books themselves, too: William Blake in London in 1789 with *Songs of Innocence*; Robert Burns, the Scottish poet, brought out his own edition of *Poems*, in 1786; Edgar Allan Poe, in 1827, self-published his long poem, *Tamerlane*; and so had another New Jerseyan well-known to Williams, Walt Whitman, with *Leaves of Grass* in 1855.

Why, even college chum Ezra Pound—now in London, after having been fired from a teaching job at Wabash College—had had *his* first book, *A Lume Spento (With Candles Quenched)* printed in Venice in 1908; and he paid for it himself.

Williams's first book was a family affair from the start. Faithful brother Ed designed a lovely title page, adorned with brief quotes chosen from Williams's poetic idols: "Happy melodist forever piping songs forever new—Keats;" and "So all my best is dressing old words new/Spending again what is already spent—Shakespeare."

He took the manuscript, a twenty-two page pamphlet entitled, simply, *Poems*, to a local printer and family friend, Reid Howell, who produced the job, all one hundred copies, for a grand total of $32.45. But when William George Williams got hold of it, he was aghast at the number of typographical errors and went through the little book with a characteristically sharp pencil. Son William, embarrassed, went back to press again, and in May, 1909, a second printing was published, errors purged.

Williams took a bundle of books down to Garrison's Stationery Store in Rutherford along with a cardboard sign Ed provided. "Poems by William C. Williams," it proudly proclaimed, "Limited Edition. On sale now."

Little did the poet realize how "limited" the book really would be. Mr. Garrison managed to sell four copies at twenty-five cents each. Williams gave away some books to friends. Mr. Howell, the printer, dutifully stored the rest in his chicken coop, where they remained for ten years until destroyed by a fire.

Poems began, appropriately, with a sonnet called "Innocense," which, in the opinion of the poet, "can never perish." His father evidently overlooked the spelling error. Williams fervently believed his whole life that a core of purity at the heart of every person remained untouched no matter how involved he or she became in the hard business of living.

"Eyes that can see," another poem, exclaims,

> *Oh, what a rarity!*
> *For many a year gone by*
> *I've looked and nothing seen*
> *But ever been*
> *Blind to a patent wide reality.*

The young man confessed to his awakening, and other poems touched up Williams's spiritual coming-of-age: "The Quest of Happiness," "The Loneliness of Life," "The Bewilderment of Youth," and, of course, "Hymn to Perfection."

There were poems about the higher aspects of life, about love, nature, God, culture, truth and beauty, friendship. They were visions of man's ideal state, dreams of romance. The poems didn't let on that the author was a doctor in training who spent most of his waking life in the raw pulsebeat of a metropolitan New York City hospital ward.

❧

Lo and behold, William Carlos Williams's first book was reviewed! A sympathetic and charitable writer in the *Rutherford American* of May 6, 1909, had this to say about the hometown boy under the headline, *Poems composed in odd moments by one of Rutherford's bright young men,*

". . . a neat little booklet. Dr. Williams has wooed the muse to good effect . . . It may well be hoped that in his busy professional life, Dr. Williams will find more odd moments in which to record his open-eyed interest in the things of beauty, the mind, and the spirit."

And what of friend Ezra's all-important response? The two kept in touch after graduation, as Pound traveled widely, came back, taught for a while, went away again. The previous spring, Ezra had stopped in for a visit with the Williams family. As was their custom, the two young poets went for a walk around the countryside. Scanning the fresh fields, Williams remarked, "Look, Ez, there's the winter wheat coming up to greet you," to which his arrogant friend replied, "It's the first intelligent wheat I've seen."

That nagging tone continued from over the seas. Pound never gave up trying to convince out-of-touch Williams to join him: "You'd better come across and broaden your mind," he teased.

In early May, Williams sent off a copy of his book to Ezra and waited anxiously for a pronouncement. Unfortunately, the Rutherford book critic was far more generous than Ezra Pound. "Individual, original, it is not. Great art it is not. Poetic it is," he admitted, "but there are innumerable poetic volumes poured out here." Rubbing salt in Williams's wounds, Pound persisted, "Your book would not even attract passing attention here."

Then, abrupt as his criticism was harsh, Pound concluded his letter with a gleam of inspiration and kindness. "Remember," he wrote encouragingly, "a man's real work is what he is going to do, not what is behind him."

William Carlos Williams had a job, admittedly an ill-paying and tough one. He had a book of poems published; admittedly no one had read it. Now, what about a good woman to become his wife?

Williams first noticed Charlotte Herman—elder daughter of Paul Herman of Rutherford, a successful German-American printer, and his wife, Nani—back in the spring of 1908. Charlotte had a younger sister, Florence (a quiet girl; Williams hardly glanced at her), and a kid brother, Paul.

Charlotte Herman was a talented concert pianist, an exotic, dark-haired, dark-eyed girl, not unlike Hilda Doolittle, Williams's college flame. He began to court Charlotte seriously, aware he was not the only interested young man in town. She had many admirers, including Edgar Williams.

Williams thrived on the rivalry. He found her enigmatic airs to be seductive. "What did she *really* want?" Williams asked himself after spending time with Charlotte.

She in turn was puzzled by the young doctor's experiments in verse. "Why do you write like that?" she asked him after an afternoon reading his poems, "I don't think a poem, to be a poem, should use ugly words, vulgar language . . . A poem should be beautiful." But Williams's poetry was the only prize he possessed, distinguishing him from the other men who came calling. He did not realize that perhaps there was not enough room in one relationship for two headstrong, dedicated artists.

For more than a year, both Willie and Ed Williams dated Charlotte Herman. It became clear to the brothers that she was going to have to choose one of them. Ed finally made the decisive move. His star was in the ascendancy. In early summer, 1909, he received the Prix de Rome, enabling him to go abroad to further his architecture studies. He was proud of himself and full of confidence. "Tell Charlotte each of us wants to marry her," Ed boldly stated to his older brother, "Tell her to choose between us. One of us will have to do it, because if you won't go, I will. Will you ask her?" Williams had an eerie premonition he was going to be turned down. Ed offered him the chance to approach the girl first; but no, he deferred. "Then I'll go," Ed replied—and off he went.

Charlotte accepted him. Williams flew into a rage, throttled his brother, then just as suddenly backed off, confused.

He withdrew into his bedroom for three days, and sulked, not eating, not speaking to anyone, until a revelation hit him. Williams hadn't paid much attention to Flossie Herman over the past couple of years, but he had certainly noticed her "straight legs, narrow hips, and high forehead." She was more open than Charlotte, and lacked that strangely attractive quality, but she was available. Williams was desperate to do something, and quickly.

He called Flossie on the telephone. Could he come over? He had to talk to her right away.

William Carlos Williams's proposal to Flossie Herman was an act of will. He did not love her passionately. As a matter of fact, he told her, he didn't love *anyone* just yet. But he wanted to marry her.

On the rebound, Williams knew Flossie was not besieged by gentleman callers. She lived in her sister's shadow. He convinced himself that she wanted him. In their marriage, there would be no competition, the way there most likely would have been with Hilda Doolittle, or with Charlotte. Rather, Flossie would be a helpmate, to support his important goals and hold back on her own. Theirs was a difficult love which Williams figured would help him find a truer path to Beauty, as a romantic poet. Flossie would serve as an inspiration to him as time passed.

Flossie, meanwhile, believed she and Williams did have much in common. They both liked literature. Why, she had even introduced him to books he had not read! She thought he possessed natural charm. They both loved theater and opera. He was nice looking enough, came from a good and well-respected family. And, after all, he *was* a doctor . . . or, almost.

Williams blundered along in his proposal. She would have to "take him as he was and together they would make a go of it," or the whole thing was off, before they even got started. He was a genius, Williams told Flossie, and she must commit herself to his efforts. He had to face the responsibility of marriage right now, with Flossie and no other woman.

She was pleased by his fervent attention, but all the same, shocked and baffled by such a tide of words. She wanted to step away and think it all through. The next night, Williams's speeches over, they went for a walk around a deserted field on the outskirts of town. Finally, and with a tinge of doubt in her voice, Flossie said she would marry Williams—eventually.

He bent down to embrace her, but at the last moment, Flossie tilted her head away, and Williams kissed but half of her upturned mouth.

Two weeks later, he was off for a year of medical study at the University of Leipzig, Germany. The couple decided their engagement was tentative and above all else, secret. Flossie told him they certainly would be good friends while he was gone and should write often to each other.

Anything could happen while the young doctor was away. A year was a long time.

~§

In the spirit of fairness to his two sons, Mr. Williams promised Willie that if Ed won the Prix de Rome, he could likewise go abroad. So that when he set sail for Leipzig in July, 1909, it was supposed to be for the purpose of continuing his medical training, to help make him an even better-informed physician. He would take courses and return refreshed, ready to start a practice in Rutherford.

But Williams was also running away, from the pain he felt about the loss of Charlotte, his loss of trust in Ed, Flossie's divided feelings, and his own inept attempts to grow up so fast, to force all the ingredients of his life to fit neatly together before he had had a chance to understand himself well enough.

The trip was a safety valve, putting distance between Williams and all that he thought was too familiar.

As soon as he arrived in Leipzig, though, he found his waking thoughts turning toward home and Flossie. He could not shake her free. He experienced the profound isolation that always pulsed through him whenever he settled in a new place.

Once again, he discovered his true interests rising to the surface. He found his medical studies hard going and preferred the courses in drama.

Williams had taken his first European trip as a schoolboy. This time, with a good deal of poetry to his credit, he saw everything through very different eyes. He saw the difference between the Old World of Europe and the New World of America—and preferred what he had left behind. "Bo," he wrote to Ed, "this country is worn out. Give me my country where there is water to drink and freedom such as they only dream of here." When Williams spoke of freedom, he did not mean civil liberties or tried-and-true democracy. He meant the freedom that comes with familiarity; the way you feel when you know where you are and can get around without puzzlement; the special kind of freedom that only comes when you are close to home and don't have to think twice about how to go from one place to another.

One day, Williams received a letter from Flossie in which she enclosed a photograph of herself, taken by a professional photographer. As he looked at the portrait more closely, Williams was angered to notice it had been retouched; the true image of Flossie was hiding beneath skillfully applied paint. He took a knife and scraped the surface of the picture away, down to the real image. He had to see her as she really was. He knew she was not that beautiful. Her sister was the beautiful one. She had not wanted to marry him because he was an artist? Well and good. Now he had a girl, at last, and he would keep her. His Flossie must never be glorified or changed in any way.

And for Williams's part, he told her, in one of his many letters, he was going to take on the medical career to support himself and his family. That was to be clearly understood by everyone. In the meantime, though, Flossie had better not forget, there was a second part of William Carlos Williams destined to do battle on a different field.

He repeated his intention to keep on with poetry: "I will not yield to please you for I love you too much to believe you would want me to be less than my highest desires." Just as he refused to tolerate touched-up photographs of Flossie, it was *her* responsibility to accept him just as *he* was and endeavored to become. If not, he concluded, in stern tones, "If you refuse me, I can and will work alone."

Strong words, threatening words, calculated to present an impression of dignified strength, and to put fear and respect into a young woman's heart.

ᏺᏣ

Giving in to his friend's repeated challenges, Williams left Leipzig for London, to visit Ezra Pound, who was looking more and more the part of a famous writer. His bright red beard was sharpened to a point, his hair more flowing than ever, and he sported a walking stick and cape. Pound lived in a dark, two-room apartment at Ten Church Walk in Kensington. The larger room was reserved for cooking only; the smaller, triangular-shaped, was for socializing and writing.

In addition to indulging his preference for exotic blends of coffee to keep him awake at night while he composed verse, Pound was trying hard to make a name for himself with the literary crowd. He took Williams to a reading by the illustrious Irish poet, William Butler Yeats. At the end, Williams waited in the hallway while his bold friend Ezra enjoyed a private audience with the great bard.

Williams found the whole experience—rubbing shoulders with the famous, promenading down twisted streets always one pace behind Ezra, endlessly darting in and out of cheap restaurants, seeing the sights of London— very exciting, but tiring. Williams was beginning to develop an idea of how he was going to live as a writer, and his view differed sharply from Ezra's.

Williams was going to be involved in a profession that would take up most of his time. The writing life would have to come before or after the medical life, or be grabbed at odd and brief moments. There would not be as much opportunity for mingling, mixing, trying to advance his reputation.

এ

His next stop was Paris, then on to Rome for a visit with brother Ed, who also took Williams touring.

But his mind was filled with thoughts of home, of his America. After leaving Ed, and enjoying a brief stop at Toledo, Spain, Williams made a special point to visit the town of Palos de la Frontera, to stand at the very spot where Christopher Columbus began his voyage to the New World. That *was* a thrill, because Williams, too, was intoxicated with the idea of exploration leading to discovery.

Christopher Columbus did not know what lay before him, but was determined to find out. That spirit of bravery and intrigue with the unknown made him one of Williams's first heroes.

America became the New World, a new place for Columbus. Williams belonged there, too; and, a year after he left home, he headed back, looking forward to a deeper plunge into the other "new world" of his imagination. His practical side told Williams he would have to enter equally deeply the new worlds of marriage and career.

During the voyage west, Williams comforted himself with the image of Flossie, waiting to greet him at the pier. Flossie, dear Flossie, would welcome him, gather him in her arms . . .

V

"*The happy genius of my household*"

But his fiancée, disturbed by the tone of Williams's letters from abroad, and uncertain of her true feelings toward him after a year's separation, decided to keep her distance for a while. Flossie was not at the pier when Williams's ship came in.

The couple needed to get to know each other again, later on. For now, Williams threw himself into preparations for beginning his medical practice, and in September, 1910, put out his shingle. His first patient was a little girl with dandruff. His earnings that year came to seven hundred and fifty dollars. He was also appointed to the post of physician for the Rutherford public school system. He wrote about the children in his pocket diary:

> *I bless the muscles of their legs, their necks*
> *that are limber, their hair that is like new*
> *grass, their eyes that are not always for dancing,*
> *their postures so naive and graceful, their voices*
> *that are full of fright and other passions,*
> *their transparent shams and their mimicry of*
> *adults, the softness of their bodies*

For the first few months, Williams got around on a bicycle to make house calls in the poor sections of town. Then, he graduated to a buggy pulled along by a fine mare named Astrid.

His first car, in 1913, was a Model-T Ford. Rain or shine, Williams's morning ritual was the same. He cranked the engine, ran in and out of the house with buckets of hot water, to keep it turning over as the weather turned cold. He worked up such a sweat sometimes just getting the car started that he had to change his clothes again before setting out on the road.

One winter night, on a maternity call, Williams slept at the woman's house while waiting for the baby to be born. He awoke, delivered the baby, then went outside, to discover his trusty Ford buried under a snowdrift. He walked all the way home.

In later years, there was a hidden advantage to owning a car. Williams always carried a prescription pad in his breast pocket, and it became a convenient place upon which to scribble notes and inspirations for new poems. He might be waiting at an intersection when a thought hit him, something glimpsed by the roadside, some piece of conversation overheard earlier, and just then recalled. Quick as a flash, he pulled over to the embankment. Out came pad and pen, down went rapid-fire words onto the little square of paper, to be transcribed later that night into typewritten drafts. Williams did a good deal of writing in his car. It was quiet, and, of course, he knew there would be no interruptions.

The car was also a place for undisturbed reflection. "Doc" Williams would be awakened at four-thirty in the morning by a frantic telephone call from the husband of a woman in labor over on the other side of town. Birth was imminent. "These are the great neglected hours of the day," Williams observed, "the only time when the world is relatively perfect and at peace. But terror guards them. Once I am up, however, and out, it's rather a delight, no matter what the weather, to be abroad in the thoughtful dawn."

~§

To get away from the never-ending pressures and demands of medical work, Williams often spent weekends at Flossie's family's farm in upstate Monroe, N.Y. Since boyhood, Williams had loved the peace and quiet of the country. He shared Pa Herman's affection for wildflowers; there were crabapple blossoms in abundance, and dogwood, daisies, goldenrods, and purple asters. At home, Mr. Herman relaxed, cherishing his private, domestic life, and welcomed the young Doc's companionship.

Williams's future mother-in-law, however, was a bother. He knew she had little respect for his poetry. "I'm proud, too—" he told her, after an argument one hot summer day, "but not about the things you are!" Nani Herman took her young daughter aside and asked her to explain Williams's daring. Her nagging mother was constantly after Flossie to get Williams to stop writing that awful poetry. Flossie steadfastly defended him, though; believed in him as an artist; and told her mother in no uncertain terms that poetry was Billy's own affair, his own business.

Williams and Flossie took long walks in the woods. Sometimes, her younger brother, Paul, tagged along. They found a quiet spot near a brook, under an apple tree with overhanging branches touching the soft ground, their private bower. While they rested in the grass, Williams read poems to her. He was a romantic soul. Flossie inspired him:

> *Lady of dusk-wood fastnesses,*
> *Thou art my Lady.*
> *I have known the crisp, splintering leaf-tread*
> *with thee on*
> *before,*
> *White, slender through green saplings;*
> *I have lain beside thee on the brown forest floor*
> *Beside thee, my Lady.*

But when were they going to get married, if she *was* his "Lady"? After all, nearly three years had gone by since he proposed to her, back in the summer of 1909. Williams tried to speed up the course of events. Why not, for the time being, renovate the ground floor of his parents' home at 131 West Passaic Avenue (Mr. and Mrs. Williams would move upstairs), set up an office there, and move in, with his new wife, until finances picked up and they could afford to strike out on their own? It would ease the pain of separation for everyone.

One night in early spring, Williams mentioned the idea to his parents. Mrs. Williams readily agreed. She would be able to see more of her beloved Willie. Just because he was going to be married, that didn't mean he should become a stranger. It sounded fine.

But Mr. Williams felt differently, and said so: "No. Not while I live in the house. No. I will not permit you to do it. It's still my house as long as I live here." He told his son he was "tardy in development." When was he going to grow up, all the way? He was twenty-nine years old. It was time to take responsibility for himself.

Furious, Williams stormed out of the house, slamming the screen door behind him. He began walking in the darkness; he did not know or care where he was going. Down the highway toward Hackensack he strode, talking to himself. Maybe it just was not possible to compromise. Maybe the only thing to do was break free of his parents entirely, skip town, move upstate or somewhere where nobody would know him or have any notion of his past life. And start anew.

He was on the brink of marriage, confused about his changeable feelings toward a woman he had been courting far too long, and about his slow-starting career. On top of all that, his own father would not even extend a helping hand.

By two o'clock in the morning, Williams came to his senses, turned around, and trudged home. His mother, worried to distraction, had been waiting up for him.

At last, a date was set for the event: December 12, 1912—
12/12/12. It *had* to mean good luck, Williams thought.
Preparations began in earnest, but the future groom did
not participate, being too busy visiting the sick people of
Rutherford, worrying about his ability to provide for his
wife-to-be.

On the wedding day, coaches sent to pick up the guests
got lost on their way to the church. There were to be two
ministers, Unitarian and Presbyterian, and one of them
almost missed the ceremony. The occasion was further
strained because brother Ed, the best man, and Flossie's
sister Lottie, had broken off their own engagement the
year before. Two years after her younger sister's wedding,
Lottie—in Berlin to study piano at the conservatory—
married a portrait painter and magazine editor named
Ferdinand Earle.

All the tension and embarrassment in the air at
William's and Flossie's wedding disappeared by the time
the champagne reception got underway. The frightened
young couple, full of hope for their future together, spent
a honeymoon in Bermuda, and came back to live temporarily in an apartment next door to Williams's parents.
His mother made dinner for them every night.

It wasn't long before, in an unexpected way, Flossie proved
her worthiness as a new wife.

If a young poet wanted to become better known in
those days, much like today, he or she kept sending work
out to literary magazines and newspapers. After a good
amount of verse had been published bit by bit, the poet
assembled the best of it for a book, a collection of verse.
And, much like today, poets tried not to torment themselves about how many people would read—let alone understand—their writing.

In 1913, a new magazine was founded in Chicago,

called, simply, *Poetry*. It is still publishing today. Edited by Harriet Monroe, it was regarded by the poets of the time as a high-quality, desirable place to have one's work seen.

Williams sent off a batch of poems to *Poetry*. They were returned almost immediately, with a rejection slip. He was more than a little disappointed. His characteristic temper got the better of him, and he scrawled a note to Miss Monroe: "I am a *great* poet," he admonished her, referring to his new works as "exquisite productions." He scolded, "I wish you well, but I heartily object to your old-fashioned and therefore vicious methods."

Williams was an impetuous man who said what he thought, even at the risk of offending a powerful editor.

At this point, Flossie stepped in. She was an avid reader, one of the qualities that endeared her to her husband. They shared a love of literature; she, too, knew what she liked and never feared offering an opinion of Williams's work. She leafed through the rejected poems and remarked to her astonished husband that if *she* were editor of *Poetry* magazine, she likewise would have sent the poems back. She then selected a different group of poems from her husband's new works, and, as if by magic, they were readily taken for publication. It was William Carlos Williams's first big break as a writer in an American magazine.

"I only wish to see myself creating those around me and within me into a beautiful reality," he wrote to his friend Viola Baxter Jordan, the New York sophisticated lady Pound had introduced him to in 1907. The idea was to move away from strictly rhyming and structured poems that were regular and predictable. Williams wanted his poems "to sound like the sea, with its tides, waves, and ripples." He wanted his poems to come "out of the clouds and down to earth, and dignify life." He wanted the shape of his new poems to reflect, in more natural language, his abiding love for natural things:

The corner of a great rain
Steamy with the country
Has fallen upon my garden.

I go back and forth now
And the little leaves follow me
Talking of the great rain,
Of branches broken,
And the farmer's curses!

ক্ষ

From distant London, as always, Ezra Pound continued to keep close watch on Williams's development and liked what he was beginning to see. He appreciated his friend's gradual shift in style toward "bold, heavily-accented metres." More important, Williams's new verse was more personal, "built up as part of himself." As a matter of fact, Pound announced, "Mr. Williams may write some very good poetry. It is not everyone of whom one can say that . . . I therefore respect him."

And therefore, Ezra Pound decided it was time for another book by the esteemed young doctor. He put Williams in touch with an English publisher, Elkin Mathews. Aided by a fifty dollar boost from the willing author, *The Tempers* was published in London in September, 1913, dedicated to Williams's mother's older brother, his namesake Uncle Carlos Hoheb.

The Tempers revealed a poet trying to break free from poetic masters both he and Pound revered: Keats, Wordsworth, and Browning. Williams insisted upon "reality" and "truth" and "order," but it would take time to bring the elusive outside world into the world of the poem. "I tried to put a bird in a cage," he admitted in one poem, "The Fool's Song,"

O fool that I am!
For the bird was Truth.

> *Sing merrily, Truth: I tried to put*
> *Truth in a cage!*
>
> *And when I had the bird in the cage,*
> *O fool that I am!*
> *Why, it broke my pretty cage.*
> *Sing merrily, Truth: I tried to put*
> *Truth in a cage!*

Pound also encouraged the poetic efforts of his former fiancée Hilda Doolittle, who lived near him in London and was married to the English poet Richard Aldington. Under Pound's guidance Hilda, too, was going through a change of style, tightly shaping her lines, each word placed like a jewel, drawing upon the images of ancient mythology and magic, as if she were under an enchanted spell. Pound sent editor Harriet Monroe two of Hilda's poems, signing them, for her, "H.D.," the name under which she published for the rest of her life. Like Williams, she found her place in the pages of *Poetry* magazine, with a poem called "Hermes of the Ways":

> *The hard sand breaks,*
> *And the grains of it*
> *Are clear as wine.*
>
> *Far off over the leagues of it,*
> *The wind,*
> *Playing on the wide shore,*
> *Piles little ridges,*
> *And the great pines*
> *Break over it.*
>
> *But more than the many-foamed waves*
> *Of the sea,*
> *I know him*
> *Of the triple path-ways,*
> *Hermes,*
> *Who awaiteth.*

ᤥ

Flossie Williams was pregnant.

The young couple realized that, with a family, they
needed a house of their own. Williams went to his generous
father-in-law and asked for help with a down-payment on
a house in the heart of Rutherford. It was a comfortable,
eight-room Victorian-style frame home, set on a low hill
near the intersection of a broad, tree-lined residential
street, Ridge Road, and the downtown business district; a
good place to live, and an appropriate location for a doctor's
office.

Nine Ridge Road had a large, rectangular front room
and perpendicular dining room on the first floor. Williams
set up his office in a back room, just off the kitchen, so it
was easy for him to pop in between patients for a quick
lunch or dinner with Flossie. He was not much of a cook
himself. As a matter of fact, he never prepared a meal on
his own, or even a cup of coffee, leaving that work to his
wife.

Upstairs, bedrooms looked out over the street in front
and the large garden in back. Williams and Flossie planted
every imaginable kind of flower and vegetable there;
pansies and roses were her favorites. Every time they went
on a trip upstate, or to New England, or to the Jersey
shore, they always returned with cuttings, and even sap-
lings, which they planted in their garden. Evenings before
dinner, they walked arm-in-arm around the garden, surveying the flowers, enthusiastically discussing plans for
what to put in next. In later years, Williams built an arbor
there.

He ran the office all by himself: no receptionist, nurse,
or secretary. Flossie kept track of house calls and bills, who
had paid and who had not. She worked out a simple nota-
tion system. A slanted line in the account-book, (/), meant
there was a house-call to be made; a dot (.) meant the call
was completed by her husband; and an X-mark meant,
simply, "paid."

In the early days, Dr. Williams sat alone, waiting for patients. He had more time on his hands than he really wanted. During one such quiet stretch, when phone and doorbell were silent, he wrote a poem called "Le Medecin Malgré Lui" ("The Doctor in Spite of Himself"), letting his eye wander around the little office and take inventory:

> *Oh I suppose I should*
> *wash the walls of my office*
> *polish the rust from*
> *my instruments and keep them*
> *definitely in order*
> *build shelves in the laboratory*
> *empty out the old stains*
> *clean the bottles*
> *and refill them, buy*
> *another lens, put*
> *my journals on edge instead of*
> *in heaps—*

Williams also completed a long poem in seven parts called "The Wanderer," inspired by his English grandmother. Williams always remained close to her, especially during times when he was having trouble communicating with his father.

In the poem, his grandmother takes on the character of a gypsy queen, a magical witch, turning a lost child (Williams himself) into a sea gull who flies through time and space. His grandmother shows him how he can do anything at all through the sheer power of his mind and will. She also reminds him to respect the living things of the earth. In the end, the boy is baptized in the waters of the Passaic River.

Indeed, family relationships were much on Williams's mind during his first years of marriage. Continuing his interest in drama, he wrote four short plays set in Colonial America, all concerned with the variety of ways young lovers encounter their difficult parents. Facing up to such problems in his own life was made easier because Williams knew he could write about them. Even though his stern father might not have been sympathetic to his financial needs; even though his mother-in-law might not have admired Williams's romantic poems, inspired by her daughter; he could still turn to the blank page for comfort, to work his feelings into words.

Writing lifted him out of darker moods. So did painting, which he continued to pursue until 1914. One afternoon, Williams went down to the banks of the Passaic, the river that meandered through town, and painted it in a pastoral scene, shrouded by thick clumps of trees, winding toward misty invisibility in the soft, green background.

His self-portrait shows us an open-faced young man of thirty-one, with slightly pointed, protruding ears, dark hair tousled atop his head, arched eyebrows over equally dark eyes with bright centers fixed at a point in the distance, shirt collar casually unbuttoned. This young doctor looks ever-so-slightly quizzical, and there is the faintest trace of a smile beginning to form on his pursed lips.

Williams gave up painting for good, soon after completing this canvas, but kept firm hold on the principles of the art of painting and applied them to his poems, seeking always the clear, sharp image in words—the poem as a picture.

ربى

Christmas, 1913, came and went. Flossie's baby still had not arrived. "He'll come with the first snowfall," she predicted; and sure enough, two o'clock in the morning on January 7, 1914, her labor pains began.

Williams called another doctor in to help. Unfortunately, they realized too late, he had only fifteen drops of chloroform anesthetic in his black bag, not enough to ease the pain of Flossie's labor contractions. Tough little Flossie gritted her teeth through it all, never once complaining or calling out, as the two doctors measured the anesthetic into a handkerchief.

"It's a bear! It's a boy! It's a bear!" the proud father exclaimed, "William Eric Williams is here! Blond, seven pounds, bald, pink, lusty-lunged, big-handed—perfect!"

It was not long before William Carlos Williams's new family found its way into a poem, "Danse Russe":

> *If when my wife is sleeping*
> *and the baby and Kathleen*
> *are sleeping*
> *and the sun is a flame-white disc*
> *in silken mists*
> *above shining trees—*
> *if I in my north room*
> *dance naked, grotesquely*
> *before my mirror*
> *waving my shirt round my head*
> *and singing softly to myself:*
> *"I am lonely, lonely.*
> *I was born to be lonely,*
> *I am best so!"*
> *If I admire my arms, my face,*
> *my shoulders, flanks, buttocks*
> *against the yellow drawn shades,—*
>
> *Who shall say I am not*
> *the happy genius of my household?*

Willie (left) and brother Ed, 1886.
(COURTESY OF DR. WILLIAM ERIC
WILLIAMS)

Willie's childhood home, 131 West Passaic Avenue, in Rutherford, N.J.
(COURTESY OF DR. WILLIAM ERIC WILLIAMS)

William Carlos Williams at age thirty.

Self-portrait, 1914.

Flossie as a young girl.

Ezra Pound at age twenty-four.

Hilda Doolittle (H.D.) at age twenty-seven.
(COURTESY OF PERDITA SCHAFFNER AND NEW DIRECTIONS
PUBLISHING CORPORATION)

Williams (left) and brother Ed,
1917.
(COURTESY OF DR. WILLIAM ERIC
WILLIAMS)

Williams holding baby son Paul,
son William Eric, and Grandma
Wellcome, 1917.
(COURTESY OF DR. WILLIAM ERIC
WILLIAMS)

Williams and Flossie at the Connecticut shore, 1920.
(PHOTOGRAPH BY IRVING WELLCOME, COURTESY OF
DR. WILLIAM ERIC WILLIAMS)

Pa Herman, Williams, and William Eric, *ca.* 1917.
(COURTESY OF DR. WILLIAM ERIC WILLIAMS)

VI

"*To be hungry is to be great*"

Word spread through the poorer parts of town that Doc Williams didn't see fit to ask for too much money for his services. His waiting room became more crowded. Here was a physician who really *cared*, people said—his practice came first, before anything else in his life, even writing—and what's more, he had grown up in Rutherford; he was a country boy, a hometown boy who made good.

You would have thought he had it all, now—new book of poems, new wife, new house, new baby, even a new car —and that Williams would settle down.

But, a mere nine miles away, across his beloved green meadows, lay New York City, like a vast, sooty magnet. On a good day, if Williams pushed himself a little bit harder and the afternoon patients moved quickly, he could escape from the office by early evening and, if he floored the accelerator, arrive in Greenwich Village a half hour later. His circle of literary and artistic friends was slowly growing, as was his thirst for culture. Three days a week, Williams made the commute into the city for classes at Babies' Hospital and Post-Graduate Clinic, to continue advanced training in pediatrics. He often lingered afterward, for drinks with an acquaintance; or to visit a gallery like the new "291," run by photographer Alfred Stieglitz. Even though Williams himself was no longer painting, he was intrigued by what was being produced by a whole new generation of Americans which at long last was *his* generation.

"Don't bother to come home early," Flossie told him. "You want to stay in the city—stay, just let me know." Sometimes, Williams did indeed let his wife know where he was staying and what he was doing, and sometimes— when he was in a hotel room with another woman—he did not. Their marriage had begun as a testament to respectability. Williams believed their love would evolve. He also had to heed another inner voice, in revolt against his strict upbringing, telling him to let passion break free. In the city's anonymous streets, Williams, the flirtatious wanderer, could also escape from his wife.

❧

One sultry night in July, 1916, after a session at the Clinic, Williams was walking down Fifteenth Street on the way to his painter-friend Marsden Hartley's studio. Suddenly, he heard the din and clamor of bells and the roar of a motor. Always alert, he turned around quickly, and just caught a glimpse of the side of a fire engine as it raced by. In a flash, Williams pulled the ever-present prescription pad from his pocket and dashed off a few lines, which became the poem, "The Great Figure":

> *Among the rain*
> *and lights*
> *I saw the figure 5*
> *in gold*
> *on a red*
> *firetruck*
> *moving*
> *with weight and urgency*
> *tense*

> *unheeded*
> *to gong clangs*
> *siren howls*
> *and wheels rumbling*
> *through the dark city.*

Williams showed that *he* paid attention to the passing truck, even if there was no one else about on the dim street. He put down in words what to other passers-by would have been an everyday occurrence. The sensation-seeker in him did not miss the opportunity to find and record one more moment shining through the gloom.

The poem did not stop with Williams's record of a scene. Twelve years later, his old friend Charles Demuth, inspired by "The Great Figure," translated it into what he called a "portrait" of Williams, entitling his canvas, "I Saw the Figure Five in Gold." The number five reverberated in bold yellow tones into the distance, as black, gray, and white rays of darkness, pieces of buildings, and street lights thrusted forward, along with fragments of Williams's name, "Bill," and Demuth's affectionate nickname, "Carlos." Blocks of bright fire-engine red crossed the center of the oil painting. It was a high energy piece. Underneath it was a deeper sense of the poet, Williams's orderliness and discipline. Thus did Williams and his friend stimulate each other to find new paths for their work.

Alfred Stieglitz, Marsden Hartley, and Charles Demuth, had, like Williams, been to Europe in the years before World War I. Unlike Williams, however, these artists stayed longer and did not yearn to return to familiar shores so quickly. In Paris, they found new inspiration for their work in the revolutionary methods of abstract and cubist artists such as Picasso, Braque, Leger, Duchamp, and Kandinsky.

In February, 1913, a group of American independent artists organized a huge exhibition at the 69th Regimental Armory on Twenty-third Street in Manhattan, to import modern works from Europe and show them to the American public for the first time.

Nobody had ever seen anything like it before. Over sixteen hundred different paintings, sculptures, and graphics were displayed in a gigantic space. The walls were hung with brightly colored fabrics; partitions covered with burlap served to hang the paintings; there were flowers and potted plants everywhere. The strange and daring paintings puzzled the art critics, who ridiculed them. More examples of Europe's corruption, the daily newspapers proclaimed.

Equally curious, William Carlos Williams attended the Armory Show on one of his late afternoons in town, driven by his endless search for new messages in new forms —and it bowled him over. He saw that paint could be used in different ways. Paint could convey *ideas*, which, after all, you could not *see*, through colors and shapes that did not resemble anything in particular. Even with his background in the arts, Williams, too, was confused by the Armory Show. He sensed "a strange quickening" within him, the need to press on with his poetry in hopes that his own effort to find a voice for still-sleeping emotions might bring him closer to what these abstract artists were trying to accomplish.

This modern art invasion from Europe opened the eyes of American writers hungry for an *avant-garde* to inspire them.

Soon after the Armory Show, Williams stumbled upon an artists' colony practically at his doorstep, an assortment of rundown shacks without electricity or running water, near the Jersey Palisades, called "Grantwood." Just as he had tried to get himself over to New York City on Friday evenings, now, on Sunday afternoons during the war years he "went madly in [his] Ford flivver to help with the magazine which had saved [his] life as a writer."

The magazine, called *Others*, was founded at Grant-wood in 1914 by Alfred Kreymborg, a young poet and journalist and his wife, Gertrude, with the financial support of Walter Arensberg, the wealthy art collector and patron.

The problems of young writers seventy years ago were remarkably similar to those they face today: how to break into the literary scene, or, failing that—not even knowing where the scene is, or what it is—how to create their own scene and make a big splash, flourishing within it. *Others* helped solve that problem for Williams. With its bright, bold, yellow covers, the little magazine became the center of a tight community of writers proudly identifying itself as apart from the establishment. They were rebels, and Williams numbered himself among them. *Others* was the first of many "little magazines" Williams joined in order to draw more attention to his poetry. "What were we seeking?" he wrote of those heady times. "No one knew . . . What a battle we made of it merely getting rid of capitol letters at the beginning of every line!"

Perhaps that does not seem to us today like much of a reason to wage a battle, especially when a real war was being fought overseas; but Williams, Kreymborg, and authors like Maxwell Bodenheim, Mina Loy, and Wallace Stevens believed they could change a tradition that had been part of American poetry for one hundred fifty years. They were quite aware of being in a minority, but were intoxicated just by the opportunity to talk to each other, to come together with people who had a passion for their art.

They sat on the floor in rustic cabins in the middle of the woods, brought their own picnic meals to eat, took occasional breaks to play baseball, and talked, talked, talked—exchanging thoughts, finding out more about who they were as writers. Williams was quick to acknowledge the solitary nature of his craft; and also the first to recognize the importance of publicly testing his ideas, at all costs to stay involved. He wrote his first "playlet in verse" at this time, called *The Old Apple Tree*.

❧

Alfred Kreymborg grew to admire Williams's idealism, nicknaming him "Don Quixote in a Model-T," and Williams thrived in the experimental atmosphere of Grantwood, broadening his contacts in the literary community. He readily agreed when, in 1916, Kreymborg asked if he would like to take the helm and edit an issue of *Others*. Here was another chance to make a statement about true quality in contemporary writing. Williams's choices for the magazine spoke eloquently of his high standards.

One of the first poets he wrote to, asking for her best work, was Marianne Moore. He had seen and admired her poems in *Poetry* magazine. Marianne Moore (1887–1972) was born in St. Louis, Missouri, and attended Bryn Mawr College at the same time as H.D., but they never met. She did not know Williams or Pound during college days, either, although all four young writers were moving along similar paths.

As they began to correspond about matters relating to *Others*, Williams and Marianne Moore discovered they had more in common than they first thought. When she moved to New York City with her mother and settled in Brooklyn in 1918, she finally met Williams. They became lifelong friends. Marianne Moore liked drama, too, and had always wanted to write a play. More important to Williams, she was equally interested in science and had studied biology in college.

Moore possessed a clear theory about the connections between poet and scientist. Both, she said, had to be tough on themselves, and disciplined in their approach to work at hand. Both needed to be attentive to a wide variety of clues in the surrounding world as possible inspiration for their work. And both had to "strive for precision in the process of discovery." Yes, the more she thought about it, conducting a scientific experiment and writing a poem required the same abilities. Perhaps that was why she liked William Carlos Williams's verse so much.

With her flaming red hair tied in braids and wound in coils high around her head above a pale brow and clear eyes, her stately posture, and precise manner of speech, Marianne Moore was a respected presence. Williams always valued her company. She soon became an important and active member of the *Others* group.

Williams liked her simple style of writing and delighted in calling her "the leading light of the Sex of the Future." She admired his "willingness to be reckless."

For Williams's issue of *Others*, Marianne Moore sent along a new poem called "Critics and Conoisseurs," typical of the style she became famous for later on: sincere, detailed, focused on little things in nature, animals and plants, the lines carefully counted out in syllables:

> *Happening to stand*
> *by an ant-hill, I have*
> > *seen a fastidious ant carrying a stick north, south,*
> > *east, west, till it turned on*
> > *itself, struck out from the flower bed into the lawn,*
> > *and returned to the point*
>
> *from which it had started*

Meaningful titles of books and poems were always important to William Carlos Williams, and his third collection of verse—the first major grouping to be brought out in America—was no exception: *Al Que Quiere!* (*To Him Who Wants It*), published by the Four Seas Company of Boston in 1917. The title came to him as the idea of a schoolboy on the playing field wanting to pass a soccer ball to a teammate.

"To get a book published! What a marvelous thing!" he exclaimed. Should he—Williams asked his new friend and advisor Marianne Moore—subtitle the volume, "The Pleasures of Democracy," reflecting his increasing delight in the possibilities awaiting a young writer who kept on plugging away? In the end, Williams thought better of it. Alfred Kreymborg was pleased to discover the first two words of the title in Spanish sounded like a scarcely hidden dedication to him ("Al K.").

Ever since the Armory Show, Williams had been trying for more time and freedom in his personal and creative life, while moving deeper into his medical practice, and snatching at every possible spare moment to explore new forms of writing. Considerable energy was flowing into his concern about the problems of sick people in Passaic County and into his never-ending struggle to find a form for his poems without ruining the native American language from which they emerged. At the same time, he was having trouble keeping in touch with his wife and—since September 13, 1916, when his second son, Paul Herman, was born—two children.

The poems of *Al Que Quiere!* showed a man devoted to his family, but perhaps more in the realm of imagination than in reality. There simply were not enough hours in a day, and something, or someone, had to give. Sunday was traditionally a family day, but when it came down to the choice between some quiet hours with the wife and children, or a quick spin over to Grantwood to see how Kreymborg and his writer pals were getting along, it was obvious who was beginning to win out.

Al Que Quiere! portrayed William Carlos Williams finding his way, beginning to discover his natural personal style; a self-described (and likewise labeled by his father) middle-class late-bloomer, with eyes opening wider, figuring out a writing style that imitated how people talked. Williams believed since childhood in the beauty of simplicity. *Al Que Quiere!* revealed the first fruits of his belief.

The book captured life in sleepy Rutherford: character studies of Williams's townspeople, snapshots of old men, young women and housewives, little boys and girls at play. There were poems about the seasons and the way they passed in and out of each other, especially when noticed by a poet with a love for the turning year. There were poems about the "smell of the earth," "the coming of spring;" two flowers, chicory and daisies, one a tough sign of bitterness, the other of simple beauty. In the poet's magical eye, leaves at autumn were changed into "little yellow fish/swimming in the river." And the most simple household events were filled with new meaning:

GOOD NIGHT

In brilliant gas light
I turn the kitchen spigot
and watch the water plash
into the clean white sink.
On the grooved drain-board
to one side is
a glass filled with parsley—
crisped green.

                        Waiting
for the water to freshen—
I glance at the spotless floor—:
a pair of rubber sandals
lie side by side
under the wall-table
all is in order for the night.

"Well, mind, here we have/our little son beside us," Williams wrote, in another poem, "Promenade," about his boy, William Eric, now a toddler, "a little diversion before breakfast!"

Come, we'll walk down the road
till the bacon be frying.
We might better be idle?
A poem might come of it?
Oh, be useful. Save annoyance
to Flossie and besides—the wind!

It's cold. It blows our
old pants out! It makes us shiver!
See the heavy trees
shifting their weight before it.
Let us be trees, an old house,
a hill with grass on it!
The baby's arms are blue.
Come, move! Be quieted!

II
So. We'll sit here now
and throw pebbles into
this water-trickle.
        Splash the water up!
(Splash it up, Sonny!) Laugh!
Hit it there deep under the grass.
See it splash! Ah, mind,
see it splash! It is alive!

In childhood, nature all around him had been there to be seen and appreciated, but Williams had no real responsibilities. Now, as a grown-up doctor, on his way to yet another house call, the country landscape meant something different when he moved through it:

When I was younger
it was plain to me
I must make something of myself.
Older now
I walk back streets
admiring the houses
of the very poor

The family doctor with a general practice was witness to life's endings as well as beginnings. "The moon is low, its silent flames almost level among the trees, across the

budding rose garden, upon the grass . . ." Dr. Williams lay
in bed, thinking quietly, unable to sleep, his mind a tumult,
a confused mixture of past poems and future lines still to
be written. The phone rang. At three in the morning, it
could only mean one thing: birth, or . . .

"Hurry! Hurry! Hurry!" the hysterical wife cried out.
The doctor was once more on his way. "Upstairs! He's
dying . . . Oh, my God, what will I do without him?" The
family doctor entered people's homes every day and night.
He sought the most intimate information in order to track
down disease and make the right diagnosis. He pushed
without fear to the center of his patients' lives. He convinced them to trust him, so he could heal them.

Williams was ever on the move. The more lives he
invaded, the more he looked at his watch in order to make
time for even more visits. He delivered babies by candle-
light, in homes without sterile water or heat. He slept on
two chairs pushed together, his shirt rolled into a makeshift
pillow while he waited for labor to take its course. He
slept sitting up, leaning over a kitchen table, head cradled
in his folded arms, waiting for the long night to pass.

Finally, by dawn, a woman became a mother. As she
delivered, Williams "welcomed the feel of her hands and
the strong pull. It quieted [him] in the way the whole
house had quieted [him] all night. It was [Williams] who
was being comforted and soothed." For those tense, silent,
prebirth hours, Dr. Williams sat in attendance, as if in the
wings at a theater, until the moment for his entrance onto
the stage.

And afterward, before he left for home, he drank a
toast of homemade whiskey with the men of the family as
the baby nursed, and the other kids crowded around their
mother's bed to gaze curiously, in awe, at their new brother
or sister.

The sky brightening, Dr. Williams drove back to Nine
Ridge Road. To sleep? If—only if—he was exhausted beyond words. More often, it was time to write, because when
else *would* there be time?

In the spring of 1917, Williams set a task for himself. Although he did not plan for it at the moment, the result would be another book. For one year, he decided, no matter what hour it was when he returned home from his daily rounds and housecalls, he would write *every single day*, without missing a day: three hundred and sixty-five entries in his diary. The physician was a creature of habit. He loved to create at least an appearance of order in his crowded life. Passage by passage, scrap by scrap, twelve months later, on sheer determination, he had another manuscript: *Kora in Hell*.

William Carlos Williams wanted to come up with a positive response to American involvement in World War I, protesting the best way he knew how, as a writer. He fought back on his own terms, "to write whatever I damn please, whenever I damn please and it'll be good if the authentic spirit of change is in it."

And so, he composed *Kora in Hell* to find out what was in his mind; his imagination, like a butterfly, alighted restlessly on many different things. In what he called his "broken style of poetry and prose" he gave himself free rein to discover a new form of writing for the future. *Kora* was Williams the free writer, letting his mind wander where it wanted.

He looked out his upstairs bedroom window:

So far away August green as it yet is. They say the sun still comes up o'mornings and it's harvest moon now. Always one leaf at the peak twig swirling, swirling and apples rotting in the ditch.

He drove his car on a late autumn afternoon and sensed approaching winter's chill, the hardest season for a doctor, the season of illness, when he had to work the longest hours. Was it any wonder spring was Williams's favorite?

How smoothly the car runs. And these rows of
celery, how they bitter the air—winter's authentic
foretaste. Here among these farms how the year
has aged, yet here's last year and the year before
and all years.

Or, he leaned over baby Paul's crib and lovingly pondered the odd actions of his new son, the way a baby never
failed to allow Williams to see the whole world fresh:

This is a slight stiff dance to a waking baby
whose arms have been lying curled back above
his head upon the pillow, making a flower—the
eyes closed. Dead to the world! Waking is a little
hand brushing away dreams. Eyes open. Here's a
new world.

⤳§

The war years proved to be a time of hardship for the
Herman family. In August, 1914, Flossie's little brother,
Paul, just fourteen years old, was accidentally killed in a
hunting accident at the farm. His son's death plunged Pa
Herman into a depression from which he never fully recovered. Soon after, Germany invaded Belgium. Mr. Herman, though a German immigrant, avoided the political
rallies sponsored by his fellow countrymen in nearby communities and remained steadfastly loyal to the United
States. But the Hermans were suspect in Rutherford, a
small town where everyone knew everyone else's business.
Their house was spied upon. They all felt increasingly
uncomfortable.

Even Williams's own mother could not control her hot
temper and made insulting remarks about their German
in-laws. Finally, when America entered the war, the patriotic pressure became too much for the Hermans, and they
moved out of Rutherford and up to the farm.

Meanwhile, sister Charlotte Herman (now Charlotte

Earle), and her husband, Ferdinand, had moved to Hollywood, California. They had two sons, Ferdinand, Jr., born 1914 (he died ten years later of polio), and Eyvind, born 1916. Pa and Nani missed their grandchildren and older daughter terribly.

Williams was not drafted into the army because he was too old to serve. He thought about enlisting, but did not. There was too much to be done on the home front. During the long winter of 1917–1918, Rutherford was hit with a 'flu epidemic. There were not many doctors available to begin with, and the draft further depleted their ranks. Williams was soon making dozens of house calls a day.

To make matters even worse, his father was dying slowly of cancer. He had been sick for a year. Early in 1918, William George Williams was still commuting, as he had every day for thirty-five years, into New York City by train until it got to be too much for him. True to his stoic character, he kept a stiff upper lip. One day he stopped by his son's office for a brief chat. "The one thing I regret in going," he told him, "is that I have to leave mother to you. You'll find her difficult." Mr. Williams felt guilty about dying with his wife still alive. He had a premonition his older son, and especially his daughter-in-law, would find Raquel Helene a hard person to live with. He was right, but someone had to take on the burden.

Never a man of many words, Mr. Williams continued to suffer in silence. On Christmas Eve, 1918, the end seemed near. Mrs. Williams whispered in his ear that it was time to call the doctor, their son Willie. When he arrived, William George managed a smile and waved his hands, a futile gesture. Williams gave his father an enema to ease the pain.

Christmas Day, Williams returned, to find his father's condition much worse, his eyes closed. "He's gone," said the son with a sigh. The father moved his head slowly from side to side on the pillow, as if to say, "No, Willie, not quite yet." The phone rang. Doc Williams dashed off to an emergency call.

When Williams came back, it was for the last time. His father was dead. He had left holiday gifts for all the family; for his older son, a small bronze bell with an ivory handle carved into the figure of a Chinese philosopher.

Shaken by his father's long illness and by the harsh circumstances of his passing—that Mr. Williams should have heard his own son pronounce him prematurely dead —the only thing Williams could do was write about the tragic experience. He began a long, thoughtful poem, "The Clouds," not to be revised and finished to his satisfaction until twenty-seven years later. "They come to me white-faced/in fear of their lives," an early draft began,

> *but I have seen my father die*
> *after a long illness and I laugh*
> *at them . . .*
> *With each, dies a piece of the old life,*
> *   which he carries,*
> *a precious burden, beyond! Thus each*
> *is valued by what he carries and that is his soul*

Mr. Williams's death forced his son to reflect upon all the conversations they never had, their misunderstandings, misgivings, lapses in contact. Now, it was too late to make amends, too late to do anything except try to keep his father's memory alive in poetry.

⋙

Several restless nights went by after the funeral.

Then, William Carlos Williams awoke from a frightening dream. He saw his father's ghost approaching and greeted it warmly, only to hear Mr. Williams's stern voice admonishing him, "You know all that poetry you're writing? Well—it's no good."

VII

"*A place (any place)
to transcend all places*"

For F. Scott Fitzgerald, flamboyant novelist, bon vivant, and self-styled King of the Jazz Age, the 'twenties were "an age of miracles, an age of art, an age of excess." William Carlos Williams was not quite so certain. *Others*, the beloved journal he had worked so hard to advance, was on the verge of extinction, suffering from lack of funds, and the intrepid group at Grantwood was breaking up.

Philosopher John Dewey, holding forth in an essay in *The Dial*, a new magazine, declared "locality is the only universal." He meant that, to get at wider truths about life, the artist must focus first and foremost upon what is closest to him. Williams read the essay with excitement. As a first generation American, he was devoted to proving he belonged here. But when he looked around, he saw old friends sailing off to find artistic freedom along the boulevards of Paris, without a thought about their debt to the native land they were abandoning.

It was tough enough for the idealist Williams to keep faith in his poems; to be scolded by scornful, phantom images of his dead father made it even tougher to stick to a true path. The war was finally over, but Williams was disillusioned, bereaved, and, at midlife, more confused than ever.

In 1920, further deepening his pain of loss, Williams's immigrant grandmother, Emily Dickenson Wellcome—the woman who had brought his own father as a boy to American shores back in 1856, the woman who taught little Willie to recite proper English prayers—died of a stroke while visiting at her son Irving's home near West Haven, Connecticut. A Christian Scientist, suffering from failing vision and cancer, Mrs. Wellcome refused her grandson's repeated offers of medical help:

> *Gimme something to eat—*
> *They're starving me—*
> *I'm all right I won't go*
> *to the hospital. No, no, no*
>
> *Give me something to eat*
> *Let me take you*
> *to the hospital, I said*
> *and after you are well*
>
> *you can do as you please.*
> *She smiled, Yes*
> *you do what you please first*
> *then I can do what I please—*

It came as no surprise when, in the aftermath of his despair, Williams named his next book of poems *Sour Grapes* (Four Seas Company, Boston, 1921). It was a moody book. The poet's achievements, he now admitted, must be judged according to different standards than those in society at large. Making a good poem was not the same as, say, putting in an eight-hour shift on the assembly line, going home, and forgetting about your job until the next morning. No, he said, "the poet puts his *soul* into his work." The poet lives with the thought of his work twenty-four hours a day.

Weeds, crabgrass, and dead leaves—rather than gently swaying, pastel-colored meadow wildflowers—populated the gloomy pages of *Sour Grapes*. The poet was a disappointed man, with "Time the Hangman" looking over his shoulder, determined to tell the world about the daughter he never had; about how "the happy shrieks" of his sons made his heart sink when he trudged up the steps of Nine Ridge Road after a hard day of doctoring; about how true happiness came only when he was alone; about a bitter sky, darkening the day after "a three-day long rain"; about drooping willows, cold birch leaves, and angry blizzards; even about the "icy day we buried the cat" in the back yard.

Even more fearfully, Williams considered the consequences of his "late singing." It took him so long to find his voice as a poet. Had he sacrificed too much in the process? "My head is in the air," he wrote, his mind filled with imagination's fickle rewards, *"but who am I?"*

At least, he still had his profession. Even with a father and grandmother gone, friends distant, family life wearing him down, and literary fame ever-elusive, Dr. Williams still understood his healing mission:

COMPLAINT

> *They call me and I go.*
> *It is a frozen road*
> *past midnight, a dust*
> *of snow caught*
> *in the rigid wheeltracks.*
> *The door opens.*
> *I smile, enter and*
> *shake off the cold.*
> *Here is a great woman*
> *on her side in the bed.*
> *She is sick,*
> *perhaps vomiting,*
> *perhaps laboring*

> *to give birth to*
> *a tenth child. Joy! Joy!*
> *Night is a room*
> *darkened for lovers,*
> *through the jalousies the sun*
> *has sent one gold needle!*
> *I pick the hair from her eyes*
> *and watch her misery*
> *with compassion.*

Most of the time, the physician's labor was indeed salvation, for himself and his needy patients. But at other moments, a fine line separated the excitement of daily work from just plain drudgery:

THE POOR

> *By constantly tormenting them*
> *with reminders of lice in*
> *their children's hair, the*
> *School Physician first*
> *brought down their hatred on him.*
> *But by this familiarity*
> *they grew used to him, and so,*
> *at last,*
> *took him for their friend and adviser.*

William Carlos Williams had been in practice more than ten years. His townspeople were used to him. He was a fact of their lives.

In marriage, the honeymoon was over. Flossie's orderly ways got on Williams's nerves. Even the way she arranged her slippers neatly by the bedside every night began to irritate him. He once confided to his mother that at times Flossie seemed downright passionless. More and more often, returning to Nine Ridge Road in the predawn hours, Williams made a detour onto a side road on the outskirts of town, where another woman at home waited up for him.

Suburban streets seemed a trap, a haven no longer, while, across the meadow, New York City's lights, ablaze with promise, waited for the poet with the bitter tang of sour grapes in his heart to snap out of his depression and come alive again.

～ゟ

Every night he could, from the time Bill and Paul were toddlers, Williams told his boys a bedtime story. But he never read to them from a book, as his father had done. No, his stories were made up. Once the boys were tucked in, Williams sat down on the edge of Paul's bed and asked him what he had done that day. Out of the information, he fashioned a tale, always of "Spot," a white polar bear, a very smart bear who knew more about life than most people. The stories always had a happy ending.

Friday nights, as soon as the boys were asleep, Williams was off to Greenwich Village. Literary parties continued into the new decade, and Williams hoped to find new kindred spirits to help fill the gaps left by the departure of Pound, Charlie Demuth, H.D.; and by the breakup of the *Others* group; for now, friend Alfred Kreymborg was gone to California.

Deliverance came, in the person of Robert McAlmon. His Irish, sea-blue eyes transfixed Williams when they first met at Lola Ridge's studio in July, 1920. The son of a Presbyterian minister, McAlmon was born in Clifton, Kansas, in 1896. He grew up in Los Angeles and San Diego, California, and joined the Army Air Corps during World War I.

He was an agile, wiry, attractive young fellow with a finely chiseled profile, modeling for art classes at the Cooper Union for one dollar an hour, living on a barge in New York harbor, trying to save his money and become a writer. And he, too, had had some poems published in the famous *Poetry* magazine. Williams liked McAlmon's honesty; he told people off without a moment's hesitation. He liked his generous spirit even more; McAlmon was always the first to extend helping hands and funds, even when he surely must have been penniless.

The two men got to talking. Williams, his editorial skills sharpened by his experience at *Others*, was itching to get involved in a fresh project to help pull him out of his low mood. "Why not start another new magazine?" suggested the younger writer. There certainly was no shortage of good work by unpublished writers around.

Thus, *Contact* was born. The idea for its snappy title came from McAlmon, remembering his pilot days, and the moment when his plane touched down and found earth once again—an exciting, suspended instant of relief.

"We, *Contact*, aim to emphasize the local phase of the game of writing," proclaimed the first editorial at the front of this mimeographed and stapled journal, printed on the cheapest brand of newsprint paper. "There is no money to pay for manuscripts," Williams and McAlmon admitted, with a touch of pride. Instead, writers should consider it a privilege to be included in *Contact*'s pages, especially if they, too, were "awake to their own locality."

Contact also meant communication, and it wasn't long before Djuna Barnes, Ford Madox Ford, Ernest Hemingway, H.D., James Joyce, Mina Loy, Ezra Pound, and Gertrude Stein, among others, found a welcome in the magazine. Williams was thrilled at the prospect of finally being able to publicize his deeply held belief in the importance of a writer's communion with native soil.

In later issues of *Contact*, Williams admitted that American artists must be nothing less than "citizens of the world." However, as they raced to find cultural excitement in *foreign* lands, they needed to take "the experience of native *local* contacts . . . with them." Knowledge of the land from which they came could only enrich "their new sphere . . . in the continental hurly-burly" of Paris, London, and Rome. After all, had American artists forgotten that America was the truly New World?

But Williams's excitement at being at the center of a new publishing venture was quickly cut short.

In 1919, H.D., with a baby daughter, Frances Perdita, was separated from Richard Aldington. She met and became close friends with the writer Annie Winifred Ellerman, daughter of the wealthy English shipping magnate Sir John Ellerman. H.D. and Annie (who adapted the pen-name Bryher) traveled to New York City in 1920. There, they met Robert McAlmon, who was instantly attracted to Bryher. She agreed to marry him, but in a marriage of convenience. They would lead strictly separate lives. In exchange for Bryher's right to live openly as companion to H.D. and Perdita, made respectable by the fact of her marriage, McAlmon would receive the benefits of Bryher's huge trust fund.

So it was, in February, 1921—barely eight months after he met William Carlos Williams—that Robert McAlmon sailed for Europe with H.D. and Bryher.

Williams, heartbroken, stood on the pier with tears in his eyes watching the ship disappear. It was as if he had lost a son; yet *another* friend gone abroad. True, McAlmon was quick to use his immediate fortune, once he arrived in Paris, to establish one of the most important publishing companies in Europe, Contact Editions. But that effort did not soften the pain of his sudden departure.

Who was there remaining to hold the fort at home? Thank heaven for Marianne Moore, still "so in place, like a red berry hanging to the jaded rose bush." Williams turned to her for much-needed comfort and criticism, and because he was her faithful admirer. "You make my blood flow in

my smallest capillaries," he told her soon after McAlmon
left, "Your gentleness makes me stop and think."

Williams also struck up a correspondence with another New Jerseyan, the philosopher, critic, and editor
Kenneth Burke, praising him generously as "the only interesting character writing in America today." Burke enjoyed *Sour Grapes*, understood its message, and detected
the talent behind the words. He also relished an honest
intellectual argument, teasing his poet friend with affectionate nicknames, like "Two-gun Williams, culture's bad
man, the cowpuncher of Eighth Street."

That was just the kind of tough position Williams
found himself taking. He dug his heels deep into the
American ground, staying home, staying put, as if his life
depended on it.

Ezra Pound and, soon, McAlmon, were urging him
to make the break and join the crowd. Was he afraid to
try Paris? As if in reply, Williams began work on two
books (both published in editions of three hundred copies
each in 1923) glorifying American places, ideas, and
things: *The Great American Novel* and *Spring and All*.

Spring and All (Contact Editions) mixed prose with
poetry, much the way *Kora* had done. Williams dedicated
the book to Charles Demuth. It held the same clean clarity
as his exquisite paintings.

Williams wrote *The Great American Novel* to give
himself encouragement, and lift himself up with his own
language. He singled out Marianne Moore in the book,
placing her on his side of the battlefield (for now, sadly,
it was a battlefield of writers). They were both poets "with
a single purpose out of a single fountain," proud of their
country.

In *Spring and All*, Williams wrote about the problem
of being an innovator, endlessly seeking out new methods
of writing. Being original, not ever content to rest upon
what had gone before, he cut himself off from the crowd
more and more as time passed.

The farmer in deep thought
is pacing through the rain
among his blank fields, with
hands in pockets,
in his head
the harvest already planted.
A cold wind ruffles the water
among the browned weeds.
On all sides
the world rolls coldly away:
black orchards
darkened by the March clouds—
leaving room for thought.
Down past the brushwood
bristling by
the rainsluiced wagonroad
looms the artist figure of
the farmer—composing
—antagonist

Like the farmer, the writer (Williams himself) was devoted to the fruits of his labor in all seasons. Even when he was not harvesting, he prepared the ground, or planted seeds for ideas. Like the farmer, the writer's work—the doctor's work as well—was never done. Like the farmer, the writer toiled alone, confronting rough weather, never fully understanding it. And, like the worried farmer, Williams, the imagining writer, was fated to be at odds with the same landscape he needed to make his work at last become real. The land at his feet was the best subject of all for his poems.

By early 1923, William Carlos Williams realized that the pleadings of his friends from abroad had become too constant to ignore. He would have to give in to them and take the plunge. He had been to Europe twice before, of course; as a schoolboy, in Switzerland with brother Ed; and then for a year just after his proposal to Flossie, when he spent time studying in Leipzig. But those trips seemed to him now like moments from another life. He was no longer an innocent youth. He was a forty-year-old professional man with a wife, two boys, a house, and increasing responsibilities. Unlike Ezra, unlike Bob McAlmon, Williams had to work for a living.

Williams and Flossie came up with a plan for their trip. They would spend a much-deserved sabbatical year together. Williams arranged to have his medical practice covered by two colleagues, Dr. Rader, and his cousin on his mother's side, Dr. Albert Hoheb. He knew he ran the risk of losing some patients who might transfer their affections to these and other doctors, but there was no choice. As for the boys, their live-in maid, Lucy, who was like a member of the family anyway, could handle Bill and Paul pretty well—at least to make certain they had three good meals a day and got off to school on time. And Ray Watkins, the Rutherford High School football coach, and his wife, also agreed to look after the boys. After all, they were nine and seven years old—no longer babes in arms, old enough to understand that their father was going away to meet with other writers and artists.

For the first six months of their so-called vacation, Williams and Flossie moved into a brownstone on East 87th Street in Manhattan. They were never more than a phone call away from the kids; and the location of the house, just a bus-ride away from the Forty-second Street Library, was convenient for Williams's new book project, *In the American Grain*.

He had been thinking about it for more than a year. True to his word, before he did anything so bold as tackle the challenge of Paris, Williams was going to strengthen his knowledge of local roots and recreate the American past. He would study the entire sweep of American history, from its earliest days, when the land was first touched upon by the Icelandic explorers, right up to the time of Abraham Lincoln. He would describe his country according to personal interpretation of the facts—to be gained from reading original sources, journals, diaries, and letters of key historical figures.

The research began in earnest once Williams and Flossie were comfortably established in their temporary quarters in the city.

"They are us, the American make-up," Williams wrote of the explorers, pioneers, and statesmen to be included in his new book, "We are what they have made us by their deeds."

Rugged individualism was a deep American value Williams lived by. Benjamin Franklin, Thomas Jefferson, and Thomas Paine all wrote with inspiration of the individual's natural rights in our society. Ralph Waldo Emerson realized as early as 1847 that "the rights of individuals were being slowly stripped away." So did one of Williams's favorite figures, Walt Whitman, when he wrote his famous essay, *Democratic Vistas*, a clarion call for personal freedom.

Williams wanted to revive awareness of those rights in the pages of his new book. He believed that the values of the "natural society" envisioned by our founding fathers, in which each person's independence was held more important than anything else, had been lost.

Every morning, in the New York Public Library American History Room, as he began to pick and choose key figures for *In the American Grain*, Williams discovered he wanted to include men who championed self-reliance. He searched deeply for a way to portray America's pure conscience of the past, to find out what were "the local causes shaping . . . genius" in ages gone by.

With Flossie's help, Williams became so involved in the book that the couple found their social life dwindling away to practically nothing. Here they were living in the middle of all the city's cultural attractions, but instead of mixing with friends, they were taking the phone off the hook, reading and writing into all hours. Williams struck while the iron was hot. After only five months, he produced a first draft.

Who were some of the heroes of *In the American Grain*? Ponce de Leon came to Florida's shores in the sixteenth century, certain he could seek out the soul of a new world in a fountain of eternal youth. He died without achieving his goal, but America, according to Williams, always was and always would be a symbol of the young and the new. Hernando de Soto also explored the coast of Florida, but was pushed back by a native force, the Indians, the first Americans, whom Williams held in high esteem. They knew how to live in harmony with the land.

Driven here by religious needs, brave Pilgrims set up the first American democracy in New England. Williams viewed the Puritan way of life as still very much at the heart of America. Daniel Boone challenged the wilderness of Kentucky in the 1760s. He "deliberately chose the peace of solitude," boldly stepping by himself into uncharted land. Despite the risk, for Daniel Boone, "the mountains were to be crossed," just as for Williams, the broad sea lay before him.

George Washington was a steadfast man who did not know how to give in. Ben Franklin was proud of his "commonness, his humble origins." John Paul Jones and Aaron Burr—one a war hero, the other a traitor—were noble, each in his own fashion. Jones took on a far greater force, a British frigate, and survived. And, much like the poets of Williams's day, Burr was "maligned because of something strange in his composition."

Like all his writings, Williams's voyage back through the American past was one of self-discovery. He sought truly home-grown virtues and characteristics, only to find many had been brought to these shores in a spirit of discovery Williams now hoped would stay within him wherever he went. Work on the book built up a faith in America he hoped would protect him.

Christopher Columbus was *In the American Grain*'s

strongest hero. Against impossible odds, he persisted in his trip while his crew and the weather raged against him.

His "insane doggedness" won out over everything. He had an instinct for detecting land. Williams wrote and revised the Christopher Columbus essay ten times before he got it just right, to his satisfaction.

And with that same determination, with Flossie at his side, his new manuscript packed safely away in his trunk, admitting to wistfulness and a pang of regret over leaving sons Bill and Paul behind, Williams sailed from New York City aboard the USS *Rochambeau* on January 9, 1924, bound for Le Havre, France.

He was nervous but ready.

⋰⋱

A ferocious storm pursued the ship for the first three days of the nine-day voyage out and most of the passengers kept to their cabins.

Not Williams! He liked to take a stand at the prow and watch the foamy waves divide on either side. Ever since he was a boy riding the ferry across the Hudson River each morning on the way to school, this had been his favorite spot—at the cutting edge, ahead of everyone else.

Evenings, he read quietly, and listened to a violinist practicing across the passageway.

His friend, the American poet and writer Kay Boyle, who had moved to France the previous spring, was at the quay in Le Havre to greet them. Could the Williamses stay with her for a few days before proceeding to Paris? Williams looked at her sadly. Robert McAlmon was expecting them to be on a certain train that very day. Under no circumstances was Williams about to disappoint his young friend, whom he had not seen in three years. At that moment, Kay Boyle understood the bond that existed between the two men, and how personally Williams must have taken McAlmon's departure from New York City. Perhaps a deeper reason for the trip was simply that

Williams needed to see McAlmon again, to reestablish
their friendship.

Suddenly, there they were: "Paris! Its frivolity, its
frantic milling about for pleasure . . . the Paris of the
expatriate artist was [the Williamses'] only world, day
and night."

For those who lived there, Paris in the 1920s was
obviously the only place to be. Writers, artists, musicians,
celebrities, and dilettantes, came together to exchange
ideas, observe each other's work, publish, mount gallery
exhibitions, drink cognac, dance, and celebrate together.
Cafes with exotic names like the Dome, the Trianon, and
the Dingo teemed with people hurriedly gesturing amid
clouds of cigarette smoke.

William Carlos Williams was overwhelmed. The first
few nights he slept badly. He had nightmares, even
dreamed one night about Walt Whitman. He could not
shake free, even so far away, from that American shadow.
The reunion with McAlmon was bittersweet. He escorted
Williams and Floss to the Hotel Lutetia, where they would
be staying. From the beginning, McAlmon noticed that
the doctor was disoriented, spent most of his time talking
about his abandoned medical practice back home: "Williams seemed lost in life-wonder, bewilderment, and torment," McAlmon wrote.

After several days, however, Williams began to relax,
mainly because he was meeting so many new and fascinating people, who liked him for his down-to-earth sincerity
and natural ways. The French found rather charming
Williams's innocent attempts to act sophisticated and speak
their language.

Soon enough, with Robert McAlmon as their guide,
Williams and Flossie were in over their heads. They met
Sylvia Beach at her famous bookstore, Shakespeare and
Company, on the rue Dupuytren; the Roumanian sculptor
Constantin Brancusi; editor and publisher William Bird
of Three Mountains Press, a friend of McAlmon and
Pound; the Irishman James Joyce, author of *Portrait of the*

Artist as a Young Man and the controversial *Ulysses*; the rotund English writer Ford Madox Ford, whom Williams took a liking to right away; George Antheil, the avant-garde composer; surrealist poet Louis Aragon; photographer Man Ray and his assistant, Berenice Abbott; Valery Larbaud, the poet and French translator of Whitman, who figured prominently in Williams's revised manuscript for *In the American Grain*; and many others.

Williams and Flossie fell into a hectic but always organized schedule. Days were spent sightseeing, unless the weather was rainy; then Flossie stayed at the hotel and read, while Williams went off to visit an artist's studio, or to attend a quiet luncheon with a group of writers.

At night, there was drinking and carousing until three or four in the morning, except when Williams felt the need to get back to work on *In the American Grain*, still in progress. Even the endless distractions of Paris could not keep him away from the white pages of his notebook for too long. When had a day in his life gone by, no matter where he was, that he had not written something?

&

From Paris, Williams and Flossie traveled south, to the ancient, walled city of Carcassonne, set among vineyard-covered hills. He was at ease there after the Paris whirlwind, writing to Marianne Moore, "Oranges, mandarins, lemons, and tasty little brown cherries in their flimsy shells are all in our yard." It reminded him of his familiar Rutherford garden.

Marseilles, the great French shipping city, was next on their crowded itinerary. Williams loved the constant feeling of the sea so close by. They sat in cafés by the old harbor and watched fishing boats come and go all day long.

Their hotel at Villefranche, on the Riviera, was surrounded by fragrant roses and chrysanthemums. The Williamses took walking tours from the town when the weather was fine; as afternoons grew longer and chillier,

Williams built a fire in their cozy room from oak-tree roots and recorded thoughts in his ever-present journal.

On to Nice, Monte Carlo, and Genoa; Williams gazed —as he had done fourteen years before—over the sea Columbus sailed upon. He strolled the narrow streets of Florence, city of Michelangelo, Botticelli, Donatello, and Giotto.

Rome at Easter time was the "ripe center of everything." Williams admired the city of churches, preferring to walk everywhere rather than take horse-drawn cabs. He crossed a stone bridge over the swift, muddy Tiber River; roamed through the tangled Borghese Gardens; marveled at the many fountains, marble ledges pale against dark foliage, and the vivid orange-red stucco of the dignified buildings. Very early one morning, he visited the ancient Forum, where the Rome of thousands of years past came alive.

After brief stays in Pompeii and Venice at the end of March, Williams and Flossie took the train to Vienna, where he registered for a month of pediatric training at Children's Hospital. He wanted to observe some of the new European methods of treatment and brush up on his diagnostic skills in preparation for the return home. Williams took clinical lectures, courses on diseases of the ear and nervous systems, and studies in the pathology of childhood.

But life was not all exams and hospital rounds. Williams and Flossie went on quiet Sunday morning walks along the Danube, had drinks at the Rathskellar, and saw a magnificent performance of Bach's St. Matthew Passion at the Opera. Williams wrote later that he felt as if he "had heard Christ speaking, had heard the wail of the voice. [His] hair stood up [when] the chorus sang: 'Crucify him!' The tragedy blew like a wind into [his] very blood."

Toward the middle of April, with two months still remaining in their European trip, a homesick Williams confided in a letter from Vienna to his friend Kenneth Burke that he would "be glad to get back . . . I have heavy bones, I'm afraid . . . there's little for me here—gravity must drag me down."

But Switzerland awaited: Zurich, Lucerne, Interlaken, and then Geneva, where Williams thrilled to see once again the city where he lived as a schoolboy. He took a nostalgic day trip out to Lancy to visit his old high school, only to find with disappointment that it had been converted into the Town Hall.

By the time he returned to Paris in May, Williams made up his mind: "I am not of this club . . . I can never be at home here." He felt even more awkward and out of place. As a sightseer, he had enjoyed himself when he was able to become delightfully lost in the sounds, smells, and atmosphere of the many towns and cities he visited. But that was only temporary.

He met some creative, friendly, stimulating people; renewed his strength as an artist; completed much writing work; even learned new medical knowledge. But his heart was back in Rutherford.

There were still more people clamoring to spend time with Williams. Because Bryher and H.D. were passing through Paris, McAlmon withdrew and was not available. Flossie fell seriously ill and was confined to her room; Williams was worried about her. One hot afternoon, he took time off to play an exhausting tennis match with a young American writer just beginning to make a reputation for himself: Ernest Hemingway.

Finally, Ezra Pound paid Williams a surprise visit. It had been thirteen years since they last saw each other face to face. They had a fulfilling talk about the future of American literature—in America. Williams met Pound's challenge to experience Paris. Now, he was returning home to pick up the cause once again.

On June 12, Williams and Flossie sailed from Cherbourg on the SS *Zeeland*. Off the Grand Banks of Newfoundland, from his favorite vantage point at the ship's prow, Williams saw vast ice fields crowding the cold waters. When the bright red Nantucket lightship came

into view, Williams sighed with relief. He was refreshed
and in touch again with his familiar New World, with
"shapes, foliage, trees to which I am used."

With the addition of a one-page essay on Abraham Lincoln,
In the American Grain was completed, and published in
November 1925.

    That same year, F. Scott Fitzgerald came out with his
sensational novel, *The Great Gatsby*. Destined to become
an American classic, it sold twenty-five thousand copies in
six months.

    Meanwhile, William Carlos Williams was walking up
and down Fifth Avenue, darting into bookstores and pur-
chasing ignored, remaindered copies of *In the American
Grain* on sale for one dollar apiece.

VIII

"A local pride; spring, summer, fall, and the sea"

The familiar view from William Carlos Williams's up-stairs window had not changed: by night, dark trees against a darker sky, and New York City's ever-present lights beyond; by day, the green sweep of the meadows. But the green and pleasant landscape no longer reached as widely as when Williams was a boy growing up surrounded by farms. Industrial progress was altering the face of his beloved countryside. Concrete roads criss-crossed marshes to the south and east. Noisy automobile traffic along Rutherford's main street, Park Avenue, passed a row of shops jammed tightly together. The once-silvery Passaic River was polluted by factory debris.

Long ago, Williams abandoned his dream of becoming a forester. That fantasy was now secretly cherished by his older son, Bill. While Williams the doctor was seeking to expand his practice beyond the environs of Rutherford, into towns like Clifton and Passaic further north, Williams the poet understood that the same pressures for progress altering the familiar scene around him were also pushing him to find a new and larger form for his verse. He

was always trying to outdo himself, to make his next work
of poetry or prose surpass all that came before.

Where should he turn for a new subject for his poetry?
He answered the question himself. As always, begin with
the world under your nose. Yet, the birds and the flowers,
while they continued to fascinate him, were no longer
enough. He wanted to use the short poem as the foundation
for a more ambitious work. His challenge, now, was "to
find an image large enough to embody the whole knowable
world around" him. The countryside alone no longer ac-
curately represented that world, but the cityscape did:
"The concept of the city, as I conceived it, was man at his
most accomplished." For good or ill, this was the direction
modern man was heading. He was destroying the country
life from which he had sprung, and his cities were sprawling out in all directions.

A city would be his subject. But which one? By 1926,
Williams had seen many cities, in America and abroad.
He had enjoyed exploring Boston, Philadelphia, Rome,
Paris, London, Geneva—and, of course, New York, just on
the horizon; a natural choice for a poem, it would seem—
but *not* for a New Jersey poet who always had a love-hate
feeling about the metropolis. New York was a fine place
to visit, to enjoy, to thrill to its marvels; but it was too
large and complex to take on as his subject.

He needed a big canvas. New York would not do. How
could a poet who chose to spend his life in the town where
he was born ever stray too far from that natural place?
What about Paterson, just eight miles further up the
Passaic? It was New Jersey's chief industrial city. Williams
had spent time there as a boy, roaming around the park,
walking its streets with brother Ed, playing hide and seek
on Garret Mountain. He still vividly remembered the
catastrophic Paterson fire of February, 1902, and the flood
that followed a month later, when the usually tranquil
Passaic River overran its banks and nearly swept away the
city's burned ruins. Paterson had survived all kinds of
hardships. Writing about it would help reclaim New

Jersey's heritage and distinguish Williams's home state as more than a place on the border of someplace else.

He did not want to write a documentary portrait or a travelogue. That was the photographer's responsibility. The poet took a subject and made it into something greater than itself. He would build his heroic long poem bit by bit, the way a city itself was constructed.

✍

And so, to get a feel for the place that meant so much to Williams, we'll retrace his path to Paterson, in late spring, past Rutherford, past Clifton, past Passaic. Trees arch over narrow roads, and as we drive beneath this green blur we wonder how we can possibly be approaching a city. But that made sense to Williams. It was as if he were hurtling —quickly, as always—out of the remnants of a green, natural heritage and into a concrete future.

Just to the southeast of Paterson, we park our car, as Williams did, at the foot of Garret Mountain, named for a secret nineteenth-century society that met in attic rooms. We begin to climb a steep trail, passing a massive, brown stone Gothic building with stained-glass windows. A parapet guards it: Lambert Castle, built by members of the industrial upper class in the nineteenth century, a vivid symbol of the city in its heyday, a place ruled by the very rich over the backs of the very poor.

We pick our way quietly, stealthily through the forest covering the hillside. It is dark, even at midday. Rotting tree trunks block us at every turn. There are no city sounds, only crickets and echoing bird calls. The forest is old, melancholy, and damp.

We break through, into an open area crowded with low-growing shrubs. The land is level here, and we have a chance to catch our breath. The sun feels warm and inviting on our faces as we walk where William Carlos Williams also walked fifty years before us.

Trees gradually give way to a wide, long meadow

bordered on three sides by sculpted trees. Far above drift three brightly colored kites, red, yellow, and boldly green against the pale blue sky.

Ahead of us, past the meadow's edge, a random group of boulders means to stop us from standing too near the cliff. We approach and climb over them, knowing as we walk closer that the sight we have been waiting for is there, *just there*.

"Once a man has penetrated the obscure jungle," Williams said in 1950, looking back to the beginnings of the poem *Paterson*, "he is likely to come out on the plateau, where he has a much broader vision than he had in the past." The city of Paterson lies before us, in the valley below. A faint haze hides distant mountains hovering protectively over the city. Paterson keeps its grip on the industrial age. Around low, sprawling, red brick warehouses, old silk and cotton mills, and churches, cluster row upon row of narrow two-family homes and rundown tenements. The little wood frame houses radiate outward, pastelcolors faded against massive brick warehouse walls. Williams heard the clatter of looms echoing up and down narrow streets. We hear nothing, except the hum of traffic filtering up from the highway—for these factories have long been empty.

From up here, this city of one hundred fifty thousand people is not without its hardened, gritty beauty.

Paterson lies eighteen miles from Newark Bay, in the curve of the Passaic River. It was founded by none other than Alexander Hamilton in 1791. He named the city for William Paterson, at the time governor of New Jersey. Hamilton envisioned the city as becoming the industrial heart of the state, harnessing the force of the Great Falls at its center.

Indeed, by 1825, Paterson was known as the "Cotton Town of America." Oxen provided power for the first cotton spinning mill in the country. At the same time, another less-distinguished tradition began. Paterson was a scene of constant struggle between rich industrialists and immigrant workers. As the factories shifted their output from cotton to silk manufacturing, there was widespread child labor and an increasing use of the whip and other harsh methods to increase productivity. Sixteen-hour days beginning at 4:30 A.M. were common. Parents went on strike to obtain proper schooling for their children, who worked side by side with them, producing all kinds of fancy fabric goods, handling as well as dyeing two-thirds of all the raw silk imported into the United States. Not only silk was manufactured. Paterson had also become a center for the production of Colt revolvers and locomotives.

Between 1881 and 1900, there were an astonishing total of one hundred and thirty-seven strikes, with rioting and vandalism, by the impoverished workers in the Paterson factories. Every single one failed. Williams wanted to write about this city, not only because its growth and decline mirrored that of many American cities, but also because he was impressed by the indomitable spirit of the people who lived and worked there for "cockroach bosses" under impossible conditions. He wanted to pay homage to the immigrants who had come to these shores at the same time as his own parents.

He remembered the prolonged labor strikes of 1912 and 1913, when twenty-seven thousand silk workers went off work to protest the multiple loom, which threatened their jobs. They held out for an eight-hour day and twelve dollars a week wages. And in 1926, when he began work on the poem *Paterson*, there was yet another strike.

The city was testimony to a technology that would have been impossible without the efforts of the immigrant people along the Passaic River. They were Williams's people—his ancestors, his patients, his friends—all inhabitants of Paterson, the place *and* the poem.

From our perch atop Garret Mountain, looking to the far
left, we can just make out a silvery, shimmering gleam:
the Great Falls.

On our way over to the falls, we notice how hilly the
city is. We drive up and down narrow streets. Vistas open
and close: old advertising signs painted on brick walls are
faded with time and weather; a street begins straight as
an arrow for fifty feet, then abruptly dog-legs around a
corner and is lost; another street stretches out seemingly
forever, vanishing to a point. We feel ages away from New
York City, not merely eighteen miles. We amble through
a warehouse district. An underground canal rushes by
beneath wide planks fitted loosely together, and the cool
smell of water rises up. Paterson's past is close enough to
touch. The mortar between red bricks crumbles. Though
the warehouse buildings are even more prepossessing up
close, they welcome us in their own quiet, solid way. Most
have been hushed and empty for more than thirty years.

The Great Falls tower seventy feet from crest to bottom,
yet seem smaller, a miniature Niagara. Just as we took in
an entire view of Paterson from one mountain vantage
point above it, so, too, we can stand, as William Carlos
Williams did, at the center of the waterfall. We walk
out onto a natural promontory, a narrow "V" of rock,
where the falls rush on either side of our feet. The roar is
so loud, thought is impossible. Spray drenches us from
below, as water strikes rock, and from above, as mists drift
down upon us in rainbow hues. One step at a time, we
inch our way to the rocky ledge point and dare to look
down, down into the deepest depths of the rushing, roaring
falls, a place where Williams came face to face with a
force to equal the roar and rush of his poetic imagination.
Here was a place to test even the bravest poet's will power!
We are dizzy and joyous with the noise.

Further along, retreating from the crevasse, we pause

on a wooden footbridge spanning the Great Falls of Paterson. Seventy feet below, in the muddy, mired backwaters, old oil drums clank against discarded chunks of lumber and rotting automobile tires.

వడ్

With the clamor of the falls ringing in his ears, and the wide panorama of the city and its colorful, violent past engraved in his imagination, Williams was ready to begin a short poem called *Paterson* in 1926:

> *From above, higher than the spires, higher*
> *even than the office towers, from oozy fields*
> *abandoned to grey beds of dead grass*
> *black sumac, withered reed stalks*
> *mud and thickets cluttered with dead leaves—*
> *the river comes pouring in above the city*
> *and crashes from the edge of the gorge*
> *in a recoil of spray and rainbow mists—*
> *—Say it, no ideas but in things—*
> *and factories crystallized from its force,*
> *like ice from spray upon the chimney rocks*

Less than a year later, the poet proclaimed in his private journal that he was going to "make a big, serious portrait of [his] time."

Little did Williams know it would take a lifetime to fill his ambitious canvas, and that the epic poem *Paterson* would remain incomplete at his death, sprawling and shifting like the city itself.

వడ్

By 1927, William Carlos Williams, the poet, had found in Paterson a new place, not too far from Rutherford, upon which to focus his creative energy. And Williams the doctor, deciding to expand the reach of his practice, chose

Passaic, just three miles south of Paterson, to establish another office, at 657 Main Avenue. He joined the staff of Passaic General Hospital, too, as it was the central medical facility for that area of New Jersey.

His medical colleagues farther afield in Bergen and Passaic Counties had been after Williams for some time to set up shop closer to Paterson so they could refer more patients to him. They felt—and he agreed—that, although he liked to work alone, he would do better if he were at least associated with a loose network of doctors who sent patients to each other when a case out of their specialty areas might come up.

Even at his Passaic office, however, Williams never hired an assistant or a nurse. As in Rutherford, when a patient came to see Dr. Williams, it was always one-to-one. An expert diagnostician, he relied upon his fine training in the basic sciences and his ability to take a thorough medical history to reach the right conclusion. He did not want any interference, any extra people around when he was meeting and talking with a patient for the first time.

Williams knew his boundaries as a physician. If he reached a point where he knew a case was out of his depth, now he had other consulting doctors to call upon.

For the five years he maintained it, the additional office made Williams's life even more hectic. The phone never stopped ringing, and whether it was a family birthday, a weekend, or a holiday, even though he might be angry at being disturbed, if an emergency arose, off he went.

On Lincoln's Birthday one year, he got a call from a younger colleague in the neighboring town of Lyndhurst, who had been ministering for more than a day to a three-hundred-pound woman in labor. Williams rushed over to the house, injected the woman with a hormone to speed up contractions, and soon enough, the baby was delivered, with a sigh of relief from all in the crowded house. But wait—there was *another* baby still to emerge—twins! "Get that first one out of the way over there on the other bed!" Williams yelled to the other doctor, "Here it comes! And there was the other baby, bigger than the first, screaming, squirming."

In honor of the holiday occasion, the proud father, Mr. O'Toole, named his two new sons Abraham and Lincoln.

Williams shuttled back and forth along the narrow roads of Passaic and Bergen counties, in and out of "textile towns" where most millworkers lived. The town of Passaic was unique in the 1920s, with a higher percentage of foreign-born inhabitants than any other American city. More than twenty different languages were spoken there, by people with Old-World customs brought over from Italy, Germany, Russia, Poland, Syria, and Ireland. Living and working conditions were far below standard. The infant mortality rate in Passaic was, sadly, higher than any other town in New Jersey. Dr. Williams had his hands full.

Passaic was a poor town. The average wage of a mill worker at the time was one thousand one hundred dollars a year. It was also a dirty town, not much more than a railroad crossing. Seventy Erie Railroad trains cut through Passaic every day, spewing smoke and ashes on both sides of the tracks.

Many of Williams's patients did not have money to pay their bills. Those that could handed over installments of a dollar or two at a time if they happened to meet the doctor on a street corner—or paid him in other ways: with a bushel of tomatoes, several freshly killed chickens, or perhaps a few quarts of potent, home-brewed whiskey or red wine.

The working people loved Williams. He, in turn, was deeply trouble by their hardships. Furthermore, during the many decades when William Carlos Williams went unrecognized as a writer, his medical case load kept his mind off the literary critics' neglect.

Williams always worked hard, and harder than ever during the tough years of the Depression. He did not want his boys to lack for anything. Each and every summer, the day school ended, Flossie packed their bags, and off Bill and Paul went to camp. They understood their dad needed uninterrupted writing time.

It came as no surprise one year, when Flossie announced that the boys were entitled to a year of schooling in Europe in the family tradition. Williams said he wanted to make up to them for the months he and his wife had run away in 1924; and, as a boy, he'd been to Switzerland with Ed. As a girl, Flossie had traveled to Germany and Norway with her brother.

She also believed it was a good time for some separation in their marriage. Distance between her husband and herself would be helpful. And so, she would stay in Geneva with the kids while Williams had almost an entire year on his own, to work, to write, to think about where their relationship was heading. She knew her husband well, his depressed moods, his flighty nature, his solitary disposition; and most of all, she recognized his never-ending need to get at the blank page and fill it with words, words, words.

On September 13, 1927, the Williams family sailed for Antwerp, Belgium, on the SS *Arabic*. Once the boys were safely established at school in Coppet College, near Geneva, Williams and Floss took a quick trip to Paris. A highlight was afternoon tea at the apartment of Gertrude Stein, the expatriate American writer. Williams admired her impressive art collection—the walls of her cozy flat were covered with paintings—and chatted with Miss Stein and her companion, Alice B. Toklas. As it happened, Ezra Pound had paid a call just a few weeks earlier, and made the mistake of disregarding Gertrude Stein's stern instructions to please *not* lean back so precariously in her favorite antique armchair, whereupon chair and poet tumbled to the floor—chair broken, poet doubtlessly embarrassed but not about to reveal it.

Miss Stein showed Williams her shelf of unpublished

manuscripts. She had developed a fine reputation in Paris as a hostess and conversationalist, and her apartment on the Rue de Fleurus was a mecca for visiting writers and artists, but literary fame had not touched her. Williams understood her frustration all too well, but there was nothing he could do. He was in much the same situation back home.

And home he went, alone, on September 24, after a week with Flossie. He never returned to Europe again.

✒

Flossie guessed correctly about one result of the separation. As soon as Williams found himself truly in solitude aboard the SS *Pennland* en route to New York, he began to write, torrents and torrents. But not only poetry. He wrote long, emotional letters to his wife, sometimes several daily over the nine-day voyage.

He, too, needed a temporary break and understood its benefits for their marriage. He wanted solitude, and he came to expect the loneliness accompanying it as part of the writer's daily burden. Had he himself not written that he was "born to be lonely" and was "best so"?

Williams resolved, to himself and to Flossie, to follow a strict writing routine over the coming year. As with *Kora in Hell*, he would try to write something every day. Even that task was no longer the sharp challenge it used to be. Nowadays, he could not relax and fall asleep *until* ten pages were banged out on the machine and could not really start a new day until ten more pages found their way into the world. First, his muscular energy found release; then came finely tuned craft. Williams's writing needed both—the burst of power, the blast of light at top speed; and, later, the detailed, close attention to word by word.

"I think of my Bunny in Geneva . . ." he wrote fondly to Flossie the second day out, September 25, 1927; and, later the same day, in a more romantic mood, he tried to capture for Flossie "the spray from the small waves . . . like a shower of white flowers."

In the morning, before arising to take a bracing bath in cold sea water and a constitutional walk around the deck, Williams lay awake in his bunk bed, rocking with the sea sway, watching reflections off the water make rippling patterns on the ceiling. He imagined hordes of patients waiting for him in the crowded consulting room. He worried, his "old bean going around inside like a windmill." He confessed to Flossie, "I am half-nervous about my practice," and about the boys, and how they were getting along in their new school. He reminisced about courtship days when he pursued Flossie, nineteen years past: "For some uncanny reason you saw through me and you saw me good," he admitted to her, "I was wild then, hurt and crazy, but that tremendous reserve of strength in me was touched and it responded." Williams gave his wife credit, but he gave himself just a bit more for facing up to himself, "I went direct to you through my own personal hell of doubt and hesitation and I have never changed the millionth part of one inch since that first decision."

The ocean liner plowed through the chill sea, the same sea crossed by Columbus, the Puritans, and Eric the Red, its "lash and slash of waves" reminding Williams of an angry woman. Alone in his narrow stateroom, he began a series of poems called *The Descent of Winter*. "This is the sadness of the sea," he wrote, no longer able, or wanting, to decide where the true sadness was, inside or outside of him,

> *waves like words all broken—*
> *a sameness of lifting and falling mood*

Once he was back in Rutherford, the poem *Paterson* grew and flourished during Williams's months alone. He wrote several times excitedly to Flossie that he was assembling historical and poetic material, laying out early plans for the epic.

In shorter poems, Williams continued to trace one of his favorite themes, the waning of one season and the advent of another. "In this strong light," he observed early one morning in mid-autumn, the lawn glazed by frost,

> *the leafless beechtree*
> *shines like a cloud*
>
> *it seems to glow*
> *of itself*
> *with a soft stript light*
> *of love*
> *over the brittle*
> *grass*

At night, the same scene took on a ghostly aspect:

> *The moon, the dried weeds*
> *and the Pleiades—*
> *Seven feet tall*
> *the dark, dried weedstalks*
> *make a part of the night*
> *a red lace*
> *on the milky blue sky*

But other poems were never even glimpsed by Flossie, or anyone else. "Love me," he pleaded in verse to his wife, in the secrecy of his notebook,

> *while I am still warm*
> *and a liar*
> *and a poet and a sometimes*
> *devoted lover*
> >   *who*
> *loves you and will lie*
> *to you*
> >   *always*

In William Carlos Williams, the poet of contradictions, faithfulness and infidelity held sway at the same time. This poem, too, told the truth: the public man desperately needed his wife's companionship in the stronghold of marriage. The private, secret man could find comfort in other women's arms.

↭

There was bad news from abroad. Paul contracted a serious case of diphtheria and was hospitalized for two months. Flossie was not pleased with the treatment her younger son was receiving from the Swiss doctors. Alarmed, she cabled her husband, who immediately cabled back that the boy should receive fifty thousand units of antitoxin.

Aside from Paul's bout with illness, however, the brothers enjoyed school. They studied the metric system at camp the summer before leaving for Geneva, so were prepared on that score. Like their father had before them in his schooldays, Bill and Paul met children from all over the world. Flossie, staying at the Hotel des Familles near the school, became friendly with European parents. On weekends, she took the boys for trips into the surrounding countryside.

Christmas neared. Williams dreamed of Flossie. But he was determined not to become sentimental during this traditional time when most families were together. He decided to spend the entire day by himself, to visit the Bronx Zoo, observe the animals in solitary splendor, and think only of his wife and sons. He ate a Christmas meal at the zoo, jotted some notes for new poems, and drove home pleased.

With spring came green sprouts of new lyric poems, and an important new friend, the young poet Louis Zukofsky, sent Williams's way by matchmaker Ezra Pound. Zukofsky had a sharp ear for rhythm in verse and became Williams's most trusted personal editor. Over the years to follow, he read and commented upon almost all Williams's work in manuscript; the older poet trusted his friend's careful judgement without question, and Williams thanked Pound for sending the reed-thin, shy, soft-spoken New Yorker his way.

Louis Zukofsky was just the right kind of selfless, respectful person to help bring Williams through the hard few months before Flossie and the boys returned in mid-July, 1928.

∾ৡ

The reunited family group spent a month at Flossie's parents' farm. Nani and Pa Herman doted on young Bill and Paul. Everyone was pleased to see how Bill's voice had deepened, his French improved, and his confidence developed while in Switzerland; and how much more bold and forthright Paul had become. The year abroad was a good growth time for the lads.

Bill and Paul, like young Willie and brother Ed before them, stuck together during their years at home in Rutherford.

It was still a town where everybody knew everybody, where people looked out for each other, and kids played freely in the streets. If a boy got hurt, it would only be a matter of minutes before his parents found out.

The Williams boys and their pals had no problem finding things to do. In spring and summer, hunting and fishing were major activities. They sat on the back steps at Nine Ridge Road and took potshots at the blackbirds crowding the oak trees or trooped down to the town dump at the edge of the meadows close by, to trap muskrats, or shoot ducks and pheasant.

Another favorite pastime was trench-digging. In secret, over several weeks, Bill and Paul and their friends, dug an underground tunnel from their back yard all the way over to a neighbor's cellar wall.

In winter, the long, steep hill down Pierrepont Avenue to Orient Way iced over and made a perfect runway for sleds. Christmas morning, the boys were awakened at six o'clock by their father rattling the iron grates of the furnace and the rasp of the coal shovel in the bin. Downstairs, the mantle over the fireplace was decorated with holly, pine cones, and pine needles, miniature reindeer, and tiny, carved peasant figures. Of course, their stockings were always well stuffed. In a yearly tradition after the holiday season, the boys roamed through town in "Christmas tree gangs," collecting old trees, heaping them high in the back yard at Nine Ridge Road for a huge bonfire.

When time allowed, William Carlos Williams was a friendly father to his sons. He taught Paul, always more interested in sports, how to throw a wicked curve ball. And when Paul resisted taking violin lessons, Williams paid him ten cents a half-hour to practice. The boy soon switched to French horn, though, so he could perform in the school band and attend football games.

Williams may have been too busy to attend his sons' baseball games—Paul pitched; Bill caught—but he always showed his proud support by buying up as many raffle tickets as possible to help the team.

Other kids' fathers went off to their offices every day. Bill and Paul were comforted that, although their dad was a busy doctor, at least he worked most days right there in the same house as they were. *He was around.*

> *Ring, ring, ring, ring!*
> *There's no end to the ringing of the damned—*
> *The bell rings to announce the illness of*
> *someone else. It rings today intimately in*
> *the warm house. That's your bread and butter.*
> *Is the doctor in?*

The winter of 1928–29 was a long, cold one, made all the more miserable by another influenza epidemic. Dr.

Williams was on the go, day and night. It seemed that as soon as one person recovered from the 'flu, two more fell ill. And Williams found that he could not step away from his writing. He tried to explain to Flossie why—when he came staggering home at midnight after a dozen house calls, ready to fling himself into bed—first he needed to churn out a first draft for a short story, inspired by a visit to the home of a sick family. It was a vicious cycle. Exciting and exhausting experiences, the daily life of a doctor, were indeed his "bread and butter." Such work supported his family. The same routine drove him back to the typewriter to keep his imagination in high gear.

Williams was afraid life would escape him. He saw importance and significance in every single thing that happened and could not afford to let any event, large or small, pass by without making a record of it.

But how could someone be so involved in daily events, people, and things—and also write about them so they would not be lost? This was the difficult path William Carlos Williams chose, no matter what the cost to him or to his family. He was reckless at times of medical crisis, convincing himself that to write, and write well, was the most important thing of all, even if he caught the 'flu and died.

❧

In the fall of 1924, after Williams and Floss returned from their European tour, Williams's mother, Raquel Helene, had moved in with them and taken an upstairs bedroom. That meant Bill and Paul had to double up. The additional household member also had created not-unexpected tensions with Flossie. But Williams had no choice in this sensitive matter. Before William George Williams died, he had made it quite clear that Raquel Helene was to be his elder son's responsibility. Brother Ed simply could not afford to keep her in his home any longer. At least Mrs.

Williams had led her own life and came and went as she
pleased. Until the accident. One frigid Sunday morning
in January, 1930, her sight failing from cataracts, the 83-
year-old Mrs. Williams disregarded her son's warning and
insisted upon walking to church without her rubbers on.
She slipped and fell onto the icy sidewalk, breaking her
hip and an elbow. She was hospitalized for five months
and returned to Nine Ridge Road permanently crippled.

For the next nineteen years, she was confined to her
room and had to be constantly waited on. Her dutiful older
son Willie looked in on her every day, brought her breakfast in the mornings, and carried her up and down the
stairs countless times. He subscribed to Spanish and French
magazines for his mother—*L'Illustration*, an art journal,
was a favorite—and read them to her. He made certain she
always had a supply of Florida Water and lilac powder to
keep herself fresh and dignified, all five feet two inches of
her.

She, in turn, darned all the socks in the house, occasionally came up with funny stories and, in her crankier
moments, reprimanded little Paul when he stole pennies
from the purse by her bed. Flossie stepped in at those times,
grabbed her son by the chin (the boys were never spanked),
lectured Paul, and sent him to his room. The boys never
felt close to Grandma Williams in the special way they
did with Grandma Herman, Flossie's mother.

Mrs. Williams's younger son, Ed, still lived in the
house where he was born, 131 West Passaic Avenue. And
so, a couple of evenings a week, on his way home from
work in the city, he walked from the Erie Railroad Station
to the corner where Ridge Road met Park Avenue, spent a
few moments with his mother upstairs, then continued on,
up Park Avenue another block, then a sharp right at the
corner and just five minutes more to his place.

Unfortunately, there was not much else Ed could do
for her. As an architect, the Depression years were hard
on him. Business was slow. William Carlos Williams—

already burdened with caring for his mother—also helped Ed through several rough financial spots. Their mother's ill health only added to the tension between them and their wives.

For some years, since their marriages, the brothers had traveled in different social circles in town. They no longer saw that much of each other. Ed had difficulty understanding and appreciating his older brother's writings. He felt Williams's style had become too outrageous, too experimental; that he violated the primarily spiritual role of the true artist. Williams, on his side, saw his brother becoming too much of a conservative.

Mrs. Williams's accident was followed much too quickly by the death of Flossie's father in March, 1930. In the same way that his son, little Paul, had been killed, Pa Herman succumbed to an accidental shotgun blast while hunting on the farm.

❧

Whenever he could, Williams retreated from the domestic chaos pushing him to write. He built a hideaway in the attic. It was chilly in winter and baking hot in summer, but it was his very own and served its purpose. When he really got moving on a poem or story, he banged his foot on the floorboards in time to the staccato rhythm of the striking typewriter keys, and the boys knew to keep their distance. The house trembled with their father's nervous energy.

In his attic study, Williams composed several essays about his hero, William Shakespeare. He admired the Elizabethan playwright for staying put and letting his imagination roam. Shakespeare did not simply hold a mirror up to nature; he created something entirely new and different out of life's raw materials. He, too, labored under a cloak of anonymity for many years, succeeding in giving vitality to a variety of characters, just as Williams attempted to do in the short stories he was beginning to write about his patients.

Williams also maintained his dedication to the drama. An intricate path—built up piece by piece over the years with rocks and stones Williams and Flossie transported one by one in the back seat of his car from the Jersey beaches and from the Wellcomes' cottage at the Connecticut shore —led to the garage at the rear of the garden where Williams' one-act plays were performed by friends. For several years during the late 1920s and early 1930s, this so-called "Tyro Theatre Group" met at Nine Ridge Road and mounted productions of Williams originals like *Intimate Strangers* and *Parisian Café Klotch*.

How he enjoyed writing dialogue! It gave him the chance to capture the actual sound of different voices reflecting off each other.

Williams also assembled a *Collected Poems, 1921– 1931*, his work from the last decade. His new friend Louis Zukofsky offered to publish them at his Objectivist Press.

Williams's verse was taking on more structure. He favored two-, three-, and four-line stanzas, a more orderly pattern to his writing, "a shape which would have a quality."

He also strived for greater simplicity, as he brought the most humble occasions into his work:

THIS IS JUST TO SAY

I have eaten
the plums
that were in
the icebox

and which
you were probably
saving
for breakfast

Forgive me
they were delicious
so sweet
and so cold

"I take what I find," Williams said, as this poem shows, a note left in the kitchen for Flossie. "No one believes that poetry can exist in his own life," he went on, referring to "This is Just to Say," always a personal favorite, "But everything in our lives, if it is sufficiently authentic to our lives and touches us deeply enough with a certain amount of feeling, is capable of being organized into a form which can be a poem."

William Carlos Williams never tired of repeating this important message to anyone, anywhere, who would listen.

I Saw the Figure Five in Gold, oil on composition board, by
Charles Demuth, 1928. The painting was inspired
by Williams' 1916 poem, *The Great Figure*.
(THE METROPOLITAN MUSEUM OF ART, ALFRED STIEGLITZ
COLLECTION)

Williams at the typewriter, *ca.* 1940's. He had written on the back of this picture, "Predatory poet!"
(COURTESY OF DR. WILLIAM ERIC WILLIAMS)

Ezra Pound, *ca.* 1960.

First draft, on prescription blank, for *The Clouds II*,
September 1944.

THE CLOUDS II

Where are the good minds of past days, the unshorn ?
Villon, to be sure, with his
saw-toothed will and testament ? Erasmus
in praise of folly and

Shakespeare who wrote so that
no schoolmen or churchman could claim him ? Aristotle,
shrewd and alone, that was an herb peddler ?
They all, like Aristophanes, knew the clouds

and said next to nothing of the soul's flight
but kept their heads and died - unmoved .
Where ? They live today in their old states because
of the page they kept that keeps

them now fresh in our thoughts, their
relics, ourselves : These were
the truth tellers of whom we are the sole heirs
beneath the clouds that bring

Early typescript draft for *The Clouds II*, September 1944.
(THE POETRY/RARE BOOKS COLLECTION, UNIVERSITY
LIBRARIES, STATE UNIVERSITY OF NEW YORK AT BUFFALO)

Early draft for *To All Gentleness*, 1944. Note original title, *The New*, and Williams' penciled comments and corrections as he struggled to get the poem just right.

Williams being "interviewed" by granddaughter Emily as her sister Erica listens. Painting on wall is of Grandma Wellcome as a young woman.

Williams and Flossie at home, Nine Ridge Road.
(PHOTOGRAPH BY EVE ARNOLD/MAGNUM)

IX

"I wanted to write a poem that you would understand"

"Okay. I'll be there as soon as I can!"

Dr. Williams grabbed a pencil stub, scribbled and squeezed one more name and address hurriedly into his ever-present red leatherbound appointment book and poetry journal: hospital rounds and twelve house calls scheduled for this morning and early afternoon, then office hours at Nine Ridge Road from two to four o'clock. The day was shaping up to be a hectic one.

He hung up the phone—insisted upon keeping it close at hand at the dining room table during mealtimes, just in case—downed a final gulp of coffee, thrust the notebook back into his left inside jacket pocket, bade a quick farewell to Flossie (who would know to have a sandwich ready for her husband when he returned), and was gone.

His jet-black, custom-built 1930 Buick coupe shone in the slant of sun reflecting off the Passaic River's oil-slicked, rippling waters as Williams headed northeast toward Carlstadt. Out of habit, he pressed the gas pedal with a vengeance, even though the first call of the day certainly was not a real emergency. A newborn could not seem to adjust to his formula feedings, a common occurrence, but the young mother was frantic as her baby appeared to waste away before her eyes. Her helplessness made the infant even more fretful and nervous.

Life along the Passaic was getting harder, the once-pristine river fast becoming a dumping ground for mills and factories that had risen on its cinder-strewn shores. Williams's dark, ever-roving eyes took nothing for granted as he drove along: the sad sight of able-bodied young men out of work, lounging against the sides of buildings or huddled near trash can fires to keep warm against the early spring chill; women with kerchiefs tied around their heads foraging for discarded, bruised fruits and vegetables behind produce markets; and on the front stoops of row after row of tenement houses, old men sat and chatted aimlessly, their lined, hardened faces tilted upward to catch thin sunlight.

"And now, driven, I/go, forced to/another day—" the half-formed lines of a new poem took shape in Williams's restless mind as he sped along. His poetry took on a serious tone of late, not melancholy and bitter like the verse of *The Tempers* or *Al Que Quiere!*, had been. The more recent poems were portraits of his times, the harsh Depression years.

Cracked concrete buildings, rundown houses, sewer pipes opening to the river, grit between railroad tracks, the whole landscape was grimy to Williams's eye these days; wrecked, overgrown, parched and washed out, where once beauty leaped forth clearly.

He called it "a cheated world." Even so, Williams told his friend Kenneth Burke, he would not complain: "I live where I live and acknowledge no lack of opportunity, because of that, to be alert to facts, the music of events."

Flash, as Williams drove on: a young woman at a dusty window with tears on her cheek; flash: an old woman munching over-ripe plums from a paper bag. It was a tragedy of the times that so many people had so much less

to do, less opporunity, less hope for work. The doctor, however, was busier than ever, at moments of pause during a
fast-paced routine speaking wishfully of getting "rid of
medicine, the sooner the better, if only I can fulfill certain
obligations and still leave enough money for bread, wine,
honey, beefsteak, travel, and a nice garden . . ."

By lunchtime, the dew burned off Williams's prized
backyard garden, carefully laid out but crowded and clut-
tered, like his own life. The back steps by midday were
warmly flooded with sun, cut off from the sights and sounds
of the street. The rest of the world dark and bare, Williams
revealed the garden's promise in a new poem, "The
Petunia:"

> *Purple!*
> *for months unknown*
> *but for*
> *the barren sky.*
>
> *A purple trumpet*
> *fragile*
> *as our hopes*
> *from the very*
> *sand*
> *saluting us.*

❧

When he entered his patients' homes, William Carlos
Williams thrilled to a different kind of garden, what he
liked to call "the secret garden of the self." Like his lifelong legendary hero, Christopher Columbus, setting forth
to a new world every single day, the doctor became an
explorer. Williams thrived on the constant promise of new
places and new faces. And medicine kept him in touch with
undiscovered territories in himself, as well as others. People trusted him, his pleasant face, quick and frequent
laugh; his nervous, sensitive hands like a pianist's.

Yes, he was admitted to all houses, where his soft
and sympathetic luminous brown eyes took in the whole
room, not just the child he was examining. He let himself be in constant demand, but took care not to place
himself above the struggles of his patients. Williams needed
their respect and admiration, and he was humbled by his
responsibility.

Back in his car, before starting out for the next house,
Williams always found a spare moment to jot down bits
of overheard domestic drama on his prescription pad:

> *Hey!*
> *Can I have some more*
> *milk?*
> *YEEEEAAAAASSSSS!*
> *—always the gentle*
> *mother!*
>
> *Her milk don't seem to . . .*
> *She's always hungry but . . .*
> *She seems to gain all right,*
> *I don't know.*

How he admired the teen-aged girl watching over her infant sister, brought home early from the hospital sick with
a heart murmur because the family did not have the
money to keep her there any longer. The child's tearful
mother barely spoke English. She clutched Williams by
the sleeve and would not let go: "Doctor, you fix my baby!"
People could not help it, they expected instant solutions.
What could Williams do, except treat the illness, then
count on the family itself to carry on? The gangly, self-
confident big sister, "a tough little nut finding her way
in the world," was a sign of hope in the immigrant household, and once Williams won her to his side, he could in
good conscience leave the tiny baby.

❦

A lovely little blonde child sat on the doctor's examining table. For the past three days, she had a very high fever of unknown cause. A diphtheria epidemic was going around the community. The only way Dr. Williams could find out for certain if the girl suffered from the disease would be to look into her throat. But she steadfastly refused to open her mouth, except to reduce a wooden tongue depressor to splinters. Williams grew more and more angry, but not so much at the child as at not being able to hunt, track down, and *see* the problem for himself. Against her tears of rage, he forced her mouth open with a spoon, determined to find the cause of the fever, deaf to her screams, blind to the parents' shock as they looked on in dismay.

❦

Ring! ring! ring! For once, it was not the pesky telephone. Before sunrise, five o'clock on a Saturday morning, someone was ringing the office bell. Williams, grumbling, tumbled out of bed and padded down the stairs, around to the side of the house. There, he found a little boy, crying and holding his right ear in great pain. Lo and behold, examining him, Williams found a bedbug crawling around on his eardrum. The boy had fifty cents to his name, but left it at home. Oh yes, he said quite seriously, he would *surely* pay him . . . later. Williams sighed with resignation; how often he heard those words during the Depression years:

> *Doc, I bin lookin' for you*
> *I owe you two bucks.*
>
> *How you doin'?*
> *Fine. When I get it*
> *I'll bring it up to you.*

Colic, heart murmurs, diphtheria, earaches—common ailments, large and small; the child's fragile body became a battleground where the doctor, driven to be victorious, fought with disease.

Success, the cure, was sweet; failure was not. "Death is difficult for the senses to alight on," Williams confessed, "After twelve days struggling with a girl to keep life in her, losing, winning, it is not easy to give her up."

Abandoned, unwanted babies crowded the wards of the already overburdened hospitals in Paterson and Passaic, another consequence of Depression poverty. The children were taken in and cared for by nurses and staff. Many of the babies started life at a disadvantage and did not make it through. Williams hated to see the little ones go.

Birth helped to balance the tragedy of the inconsolable mother, her tear-filled eyes shrouded with purple shadows, and the brave father attempting to hold his head high when he received news of his child's passing.

The joy of birth after birth came more quickly, and Williams reveled in the sight of

> *the new baby of Mr. and Mrs.*
> *Krantz which cannot*
>
> *for the fat of its cheeks*
> *open well its eyes*

His maternity caseload grew to be so heavy, his schedule so crowded during the 1930s, that Williams gave up his traditional Friday night excursions into Greenwich Village. His social life faded out. So did his already limited travel plans. When he had five women coming to full term within a week, it was difficult to slip away to Flossie's uncle's farm in Vermont, or to her parent's place upstate.

Since the late 1920s, Williams had been making rough notes for a biography of Flossie. He wanted to pay tribute to her, and to the entire Herman family. He was closer to them at times than to his own family. He still keenly felt the loss of Pa Herman, and even Nani, with her harsh and demanding ways, was a source of amusement. In a novel, he would paint a character sketch of Nani and the rest, for all to see.

The novel would tell the story of Flossie's life from her birth in New York City, the Hermans' move to Rutherford at the turn of the century, up through her marriage in 1912 to the young doctor, and the birth of her children. It would also give Williams a chance to write even more about babies. His life was filled with them, day and night; "each time they awake from sleep it is as if they were just born." They seemed like little flowers just opening, filling the room with their strength of will, completely careless about what adults thought—defiant! Williams was saying to himself with every baby he cared for during the busy years of the 1920s and 1930s, "Carry on, because I'm going to write you down!"

It was an original idea, a book beginning with the central character an infant growing into toddlerhood. Williams was sure he was the man to do the job. After all, what writer knew the subject better than he?

And so, *White Mule* took shape. Baby Flossie first saw light on April 18, 1890, a spring day, in a brownstone on 104th Street in Manhattan, in the shadow of the elevated railroad, so close to the trains that the house shook with their passing. She was a scrawny little thing, and stubborn from the first, curious and smart. Her golden yellow hair, "curled up in the center of her back like a drake's tail," made a sharp contrast to older sister Charlotte's dark hair and complexion. And her sunny disposition was the opposite of Lottie's brooding nature.

They were the daughters of Paul and Nani Herman, immigrants from Silesia in Germany. In his novel, Williams changed their names to "Joe and Gurlie Stecher."

Paul Herman began his career as a journeyman printer,
a hard-working, nostalgic man who often thought back to
quiet days spent as a boy in the Black Forest. Like his
future son-in-law, he, too, once wanted to be a forester.
Now, here he was in the bustling, overwhelming "New
World" of America, seeking to support a family and still
maintain a sense of dignity. His little daughter was the
prize of his life; and Flossie, on her part, grew up especially close to her father. She felt near to him in a way she
never did with her outspoken and ambitious mother.
Flossie feared Nani and never really confided in her.

When baby Flossie began to learn to walk, she did
not allow anyone to stand next to her and help her. She
had to figure out for herself this new way of getting
around. When toddler Flossie wanted to take a walk on the
grass in the park and pick flowers—she loved them so—
no one was permitted to take the blooms away from her.
When Flossie first learned what shoes were, she took them
off and put them on, over and over again, brushing away
her mother's interfering hands. She was impatient to grow
up. She looked to the future with wonderment, "her little
eyes full of dreams . . . and her high, little voice that loved
to prattle."

Nani was dissatisfied with her husband's lack of
progress in his job. She always said he was lucky to have
found a woman like her. Why wasn't he bringing home
more money? "We've got to move up in the world," she
said to Pa when he came home every night. And she also
did not like their apartment. Why did they have to live
in a place that was so crowded and small, hot in summer—as only New York City summers could be—and
cold in winter? "Mother Nature, that's what we need,"
she kept nagging her husband. She could never rest easy
with the way things were. She was always seeking change.
Motherhood frustrated her, being cooped up all day in the
house with her girls, even though—not wanting to bow
down to anyone—she hired maids to help out.

At holiday time, especially Christmas, both sides of

the Herman family gathered to celebrate. A constant stream of kindly aunts and uncles paraded through their little flat. Nani stood off to the side, keeping an eagle eye on Pa, making sure he did not drink too much of his beloved beer, smoke too many of his cherished cigars, or share too many tales of the old country.

Pa finally realized his dream, breaking away from laboring for other people to set up his own printing business, but the price of independence was high. The big, union-run shops felt threatened by this immigrant upstart. He had trouble finding dependable suppliers for paper and ink, and for fear of sabotage, was forced to keep the location of his new place of business a secret. Pa quickly caught on to the American Way: "Everyone wants to beat the next one," he said. He wanted to make money honestly, to buck the tide of corruption. No amount of Nani's pestering was going to change *that*.

Pa gained respect among his fellow workers. They saw him as a person destined to go up in life. He was moved to succeed and push out of poverty, because he wanted his girls to have freedom to find the best.

And so, finally, with Pa's business established, the Hermans moved out of New York City to a small country town just across the river: Rutherford, New Jersey. Now Nani could have new worries: about what the neighbors thought, about whether the dress the woman next door was wearing was nicer than hers, or about whether she should really speak her mind at the next meeting of the school board, town social club, or Presbyterian Church committee.

Like William Carlos Williams's father, Pa Herman commuted every day by train into the city to work and spent even longer hours with his growing business, trying to maintain the life to which his family had become accustomed: good schools for the girls and piano lessons for Lottie, who was developing into a fine musician; a house in the country, a farm upstate for weekends and summers.

Nani's long-standing wish came true. In 1900, a third child was born, this time a boy, little Paul.

And Flossie soon met the local kids, including two brothers, Willie and Ed Williams.

White Mule began simply enough as Williams's gentle tribute to the vitality of babies, his favorite subject, and to one particular baby, Flossie. It grew and grew into a three-novel saga. Williams worked on the following two books, *In the Money* and *The Build-up*, into the 1950s. The books became the story of an immigrant family struggling to adjust to American life.

As he proceeded in the novels, Williams wrote admiringly of his late father-in-law, realizing how much he still identified with Pa's career and family ups and downs, and with his urge to be free, *and* fair and square at the same time. Williams also accepted the fact that men often needed strong women like Nani to keep them going. Like the popular, Depression-era "White Mule" whiskey, which had given Williams the idea for his title, Nani packed a powerful punch. And Flossie inherited her mother's spirited nature, as well as her father's sensitivity.

One by one, chapters of *White Mule* appeared in literary magazines during the 1930s. Williams was proud of the book, his first serious novel, and naturally enough wanted to see it published as a whole. Once again, matchmaker friend Ezra Pound was responsible for making Williams's dream come true. It happened like this:

In January, 1934, Williams received a letter from a Harvard undergraduate named James Laughlin asking if the poet would like to submit new work to the magazine he edited at college, the *Advocate*. Williams of course said yes, as he always did to requests for his work, especially when they came from "the kids," younger writers and editors. He was their tireless champion, firmly believing his generation had a responsibility to pull the next one along.

The two men got to corresponding. It turned out that

Laughlin, a young man of independent means, had studied at the "Ezuversity" in Rapallo, and received a letter of introduction from Pound to Williams. Pound further instructed Laughlin in no uncertain terms that the best thing he could possibly do with his wealth was to start a publishing company, seek out the finest American writers, and bring them to the public's broader attention.

Laughlin was already familiar with Williams's writing. While still a schoolboy at Choate, before coming to Harvard, he took literature courses from the renowned writer, translator, and critic Dudley Fitts, who had several of Williams's books on his shelves. Laughlin recalled especially the strong impression of *In the American Grain*, his personal favorite, *The Tempers*, and *Al Que Quiere!*. He was struck by the way Williams took on modern details of life in a plain-speaking style.

When Laughlin, the shy student, made the trip out to Rutherford, he found Williams to be receptive and warm, a good listener, who put the younger man at ease and quickly relaxed his self-consciousness about being in the presence of a seasoned author. Williams was modest about his work in progress. He passed some new poems, the result of hard labor, casually across the living room table to Laughlin with the comment, "Here's something I just turned out. What do you think of it?" Their conversations covered wide territory: Williams's medical cases were on his mind most of the time, and so were his two boys, just about Laughlin's age—Bill at Williams College, Paul having followed in his father's footsteps, to Penn. They also spoke of other poets currently on the scene, and Williams critiqued Laughlin's own poems. The two became immediate friends.

Laughlin followed Ezra Pound's advice. He founded his own publishing company, New Directions; and in June, 1937, he brought out *White Mule*, in a sparkling, pure white cover, to widespread critical praise. With a few exceptions, he continued to take on all of William Carlos Williams's work over the following twenty-five years, and to this day remains Williams's publisher and literary executor.

James Laughlin did not edit or seek to change Williams's writing. When he accepted any book, it was because he considered it completely worthy. New Directions stood for literary freedom, the writer's most prized possession.

~§

Williams wrote *White Mule*, and the two novels that followed it, in order to get back in touch with Flossie, her family, and a past that no longer was. During his middle years he also found the need to regain contact with his father—gone since 1918, but still vivid in memory—and his mother, living upstairs in the same house, but a fragile shadow of her former self.

It was less painful to call his parents by different names in a poem. Williams's father became *Adam*, who "left behind/all the curious memories that come/with shells and hurricanes . . . And the Latin ladies admired him" back in those early days in the tropics, where he was an Englishman who never lived for long in England. William George Williams, his troubled son recalled eighteen years after his passing, died "without a murmur, silently/a desperate, unvarying silence/to the unhurried last." Words that never passed between them still hovered unspoken in Williams's memory, as he grew older.

His father was *Adam*, and his crippled, nearly-blind mother became *Eve* in the poet's imagination of her. He begged her forgiveness. "I sometimes detect in your face," he wrote, "a puzzled pity for me/your son . . . I have been a fool—/(and remain a fool) . . ."

His father took wisdom to his grave that Williams would never be able to regain. His mother, Williams believed, failed to understand what drove him to write and live the hurried life he led; but perhaps that was partly his fault for not taking the time to sit down and explain himself to her more often.

Williams decided there was still time to make amends. He turned his attention to the future, and his sons. He resolved to become a better father. The boys were moving out of the house, their lives inevitably becoming more of a mystery: "Bill, the older, is away at college, so I don't know as much about him as I used to think I used to," he confided sadly to his friend, the painter Marsden Hartley.

While the boys were still in high school, in the late 1920s, talk around the dinner table had focused upon their father's medical practice. Williams took phone calls during meals, so Bill and Paul had heard at first hand all the details of this pregnancy or that sprained ankle or stomach upset, this birth or that death. Williams had not shared his writing with the boys, only with Flossie. It wasn't until Bill entered Williams College—and heard other students complaining they had to read certain works by a difficult poet named William Carlos Williams—that he realized the true depth of his father's life in literature.

Despite his father's hope that life would be more clear-cut for the two boys than it had been for him, young Bill Williams reached a crossroads midway through college. Like his father before him, he was torn between a career as a forester and a writer—he produced short stories, essays, and character-sketches of friends—and the promptings of his more practical side, his deep, abiding fascination with science.

William Carlos Williams understood all too well what his elder son was going through. "You seem not far different from what I was myself at your age," he told Bill, thinking back to undergraduate days at Penn thirty years before, "Everything seems upside down and one's self the very muck under one's foot . . . Your difficulties arise from a lack of balance in your daily life," the father went on to the son, again, thinking of his own past problems, "which has to be understood to be withstood—for it cannot be avoided."

Williams's advice to Bill was, simply, to "wait, with

the only kind of faith I have ever recognized, the faith that says I wanna know! I wanna know!"

He tried to give his son the confidence to keep an open mind and face the coming senior year at Williams College with bravery and above all else with "a smile. That's what they mean when they speak of humor."

His father did not push young Bill either way. He stepped back and allowed a decision to come forth naturally. On his side, Bill knew his father and mother would stand by him no matter what path he chose.

The spirit of a physician's life ran deep in William Eric, deeper than he realized, and he went on to Cornell Medical School in New York City. This time, history had luckily been allowed to repeat itself, in a way destined to become a blessing to William Carlos Williams in old age.

X

"The war is the first and only thing in the world today."

William Carlos Williams hoped against hope that America could stay out of World War II, even as its rumblings, far off in Europe, seemed to grow louder.

"What should the artist *be* today? What *must* he be? What can he *do*? To what *purpose*?" the troubled Williams asked himself. Surely he could fight the good fight where he had always lived, on the home front, as a writer. He reasoned that "after a while they will run out of bombs. Then they will need something to fall back on: today. Only an artist can invent it." Williams knew there was no way he could turn the other cheek and pretend the conflict did not exist. World leaders had abused their mighty powers to unleash against each other all the forces of destruction at their disposal. All the more reason for artists and writers to call upon their creative energies and fight back by bringing beauty into the world. "War destroys, art creates," he declared, and although *Paterson* remained stalled for the time being, Williams did manage to assemble the finest collection of his work to date, a book of poems called *The Wedge*, with the help of Louis Zukofsky.

As a physician, too, Williams brought life into the world even as death ruled elsewhere. He hoped the future generation might live free from strife. There was new-born life in the hospital delivery room, and newborn beauty in verse:

> *She loves you*
> *she says. Believe it*
> *—tomorrow.*
>
> *But today*
> *the particulars*
> *of poetry*
>
> *that difficult art*
> *require*
> *your whole attention*

Ezra Pound was more certain than William Carlos Williams about the poet's role in wartime. He, too, was concentrating on an epic, *The Cantos*, a life's work intended to account for all his major ideas in poetic form. And he was making more headway with it than Williams was with *Paterson*. But beyond attending to creative work, the poet—according to Pound—needed to speak out, loudly and clearly, against war's injustices, seeking the widest possible audience he could find. He could not limit himself to complaints before small groups, or intimate letters to acquaintances. The poet must speak "not [just] with regard to *this* war, but in protest against a system which creates one war after another."

With that goal in mind, and convinced, as always, that he was ordained to follow his conscience wherever it led him, Pound made a secret visit to the United States in the spring of 1939, "to protest," as he put it, "against particular forces then engaged in trying to create war and to make sure that the USA should be dragged into it." He went straight to Washington and was found wandering through the Capitol building's corridors trying to set up interviews with legislators, but with little result.

Williams and Pound met briefly at the home of a mutual friend in Washington. Williams tried hard to overlook Pound's preaching, because he still had high respect for him as a master of language and owed so much to Pound, as did many other writers. But after years of separation, the distance between them was difficult to make up. When Pound spent a night at Nine Ridge Road in June, 1939, before his return to Italy, the atmosphere was very strained. Paul Williams, just graduated from college and on his way to Harvard Business School in the fall, was at home, and Pound lectured the young man condescendingly: Didn't he realize that the bankers of the world were the real cause of war? Pound criticized President Roosevelt and praised Mussolini's Fascist leadership in Italy.

Bearded, casually dressed, his whining voice booming across the living room, Pound sprawled on the couch all evening and held forth to Williams, Flossie, and Paul. Williams found, in addition, that his old college chum had "acquired a habit of avoiding the question at issue when he is pressed for a direct answer." They may have been blood-brothers in their continuing dedication to the cause of American poetry, but the emotional gap between them was widening.

౼ఢ

"Green is a solace," wrote Williams in one of his wartime poems, "Burning the Christmas Greens," and went on, "a promise of peace, a fort/against the cold." In another poem written during the war, "Raleigh Was Right," he also reflected on the importance of keeping in touch with country life:

> *it was long ago!*
> *long ago! when country people*

> *would plow and sow with*
> *flowering minds and pockets*
> *at ease—*
> *if ever this were true.*

Two forces in William Carlos Williams kept him going when all else failed: his love of nature, and his faith in friendship.

True, he had temporarily lost Ezra, but he would regain him some day. As if to even the balance, Williams and Flossie found two important new friends, Charles and Theresa Abbott. He was librarian at the Lockwood Library of the University of Buffalo in upstate New York. Back in 1936, Abbott had the original idea to begin collecting manuscripts of living poets and writers, so that students and scholars could learn from examining first drafts and rough notes for finished works.

Williams replied to Abbott's request for manuscripts in an off-handed way, saying the librarian was welcome to the "junk," as he called it. But a personal visit from Abbott quickly changed Williams's attitude. The two men took an immediate liking to one another. Williams was convinced of the potential value of his manuscripts to the all-important next generation. Anything to help them get at the heart of the poem's mystery was fine by him.

Abbott's open invitation to send manuscripts and worksheets accepted—boxes and boxes of them arrived at Buffalo over the next twenty-five years, as Williams cleaned out his attic—the Williamses were then pleased to accept an invitation in 1940 to come and visit the Abbotts at Gratwick Highlands. This was Mrs. Abbott's four-hundred-acre family estate, built by her parents at the turn of the century in Pavilion, New York, sixty miles east of Buffalo, in the Genesee Valley.

It was paradise, Williams's dream come true. How he longed to get away, just temporarily, from the intensity of Rutherford life. Gratwick Highlands was the answer to his prayers. The central manor, with its eighteen-thousand-

book library—the Big House, as it was familiarly called—
was nestled among other, smaller houses. It was surrounded
by a stone chapel; a formal, walled garden with tree
peonies, fruit trees and stately elms; a sunken garden with
lily ponds; Charles Abbott's pride and joy, his vegetable
patch, filled to bursting with herbs, salad greens, tomatoes,
and berries; a pool, tennis courts, a greenhouse, and stables.
Intricate masonry paths and roadways meandered throughout the estate. A multitude of different birds, robins, cat-
birds, cardinals, thrashers, chickadees, orioles, and thrushes
sang constantly. Dorset sheep roamed freely on the lawns.
It was a sanctuary from the rest of the world. One memor-
able night, Williams fell asleep in a cot set up for him on
the screened-in porch of the Big House. It rained, and the
water rushed down a drainpipe near his head. The sound
spoke eloquently, peacefully, of a life Williams hoped
would await him in old age.

   In 1941, Williams and Flossie took another important
trip, their first ever by plane, to San Juan, Puerto Rico, by
way of Puerto Plata. He thrilled to the vista opening up
majestically to him above the "puffs of white cloud, their
shadows ten thousand feet below [him] on the turquoise
sea, definitely turquoise above the reefs invading the ultra-
marine of the deepest water."

   At Port au Prince, Haiti, Williams saw, in his mind's
eye, his namesake Uncle Carlos Hoheb fleeing to Panama
sixty years before. Puerto Rico was his mother's ancestral
home. Spanish blood ran through Williams's American
veins. Before it was too late, he had to get close as possible
to the source of that blood-tie.

~§

The silence between Pound and Williams grew longer.
Then, one afternoon in July, 1941, Flossie came rushing
home from the bank with a chilling story. One of the
tellers asked her if Doc Williams knew anyone by the

name of Ezra Pound in Italy. Why? Because the night
before, the unsuspecting man, while casually twisting the
dials of his short wave radio, had picked up a signal from
the Rome Radio American Hour. It was Ezra Pound,
carrying on about the blunders of President Roosevelt and
the rebels in Spain; and the wonders of Fascism, the bril-
liance of Italy's Mussolini and Germany's Hitler. During
these emotional statements, according to the bank teller,
Pound asserted that "ol' Doc Williams of Rutherford, New
Jersey would understand" what he was talking about.

Soon after, an FBI agent, pursuing the case of Ezra
Pound, called on a shaken William Carlos Williams at his
office: "Are you a loyal American citizen?" the agent
asked. "Of course I'm a loyal American citizen," Williams
replied, flustered. He was sadly, helplessly annoyed at his
distant and irresponsible friend, "I-I-I've spent my whole
life, generally speaking, for my country, trying to serve it
in every way I know how."

William Carlos Williams' faithfulness to America,
called into question! He could not believe his ears. Hadn't
the countless poems, stories, novels, and essays he had
written, each in its own individual way glorified his country through the direct, plain language of its people?
Hadn't he recently written an entire opera, *The First
President*, in praise of George Washington as "the blameless leader, the great emblem," the statesman who
"dreamed of his country night and day . . . worked for
America, body and soul"? And hadn't he steadfastly stayed
on home ground, while others—Ezra chief among them—
sought freedom elsewhere, running off to other countries?

Williams's patriotism doubted was bad enough. But
that it should come about in this way, to be betrayed by
Ezra himself! "He *was* a friend," Williams told Robert
McAlmon, "I feel sick over him at times."

In 1943, an American court indicted Ezra Pound for
treason because of his broadcasts. He continued to make
them. "You are not going to win this war," he raged.

"None of our best minds ever thought you could win it. You never had a chance in this war."

ക്ষ

No fewer than four doctors in the Rutherford area were drafted, forcing the already-overburdened William Carlos Williams to double up on his work. Seven day stretches, mornings at the Passaic Hospital, afternoons on house calls, evenings at Nine Ridge Road for office visits, were not uncommon. In addition, Williams, who could never say no, agreed to take over the entire practice of a young colleague in Passaic who was going into the army. He compressed that work into Tuesday afternoons, convincing himself that it was the patriotic thing to do, his contribution to the war effort, to roll up his sleeves and pitch in.

Williams was too old to don a uniform and ship out to join G.I.'s on the muddy battlefields of Europe; but he volunteered to conduct physical exams for Army recruits, proud of himself when on one occasion he processed twenty men within an hour.

House calls continued, as before: The elderly Italian couple spoke hardly any English. The old man let Williams into their modest frame house, past the tiny vegetable garden in front, and up the stairs, to where his wife lay in bed. She had been there several days; was she ill, or not? Could she get up? Williams listened to her heart and felt her abdomen. He pronounced her tired, but healthy.

The grateful husband followed Williams out into the sunshine. They stood in silence together for a while. Conversation was impossible. The old man had no money. Instead, he pressed a gift into the doctor's palm, a silver snuff box, smooth and shining dully with age, engraved with a picture of a woman reclining among flowers.

A worker from the General Bearings Company in Jersey City, handling inflammable cleaning fluid at the factory, was caught by a bright flash and a sudden blaze.

He smelled burned hair, singed eyebrows, and cloth afire.
Even his gloves were burning. The young man complained
to Doc Williams that after a casual examination of his
wounds, the factory nurse made him go back to work. Yes,
she took him off the dangerous job he had been doing, but
now, with the use of only one arm, the other badly burned,
he was lugging forty-pound cases of machinery across the
warehouse floor. Williams, furious, telephoned the factory,
and in no uncertain terms bawled out the negligent nurse.
How *dare* she!

Epidemics and viruses held sway, in those days before
wonder drugs: the virus pneumonitis, its intensive cough-
ing fits leading often to ruptured lungs; the strep throat
infection raging through town in the fall of 1942, striking
both children and adults with few warning signs except
fatigue.

And always there were the maternity cases, first
glimmers of a wartime baby boom; at one point in November, 1942, Williams counted no less than fourteen preg-
nancies reaching full term over a period of two weeks.

Like brother Bill, Paul Williams possessed talent and am-
bition as a writer, composing poems and short stories in
unabashed imitation of his father's style. For several years
during college and after, he considered careers in medicine, journalism, and advertising. But the combined tradi-
tions of salesmanship (no doubt influenced by grandfather
William George's legacy) and professionalism (through
his dad) led Paul to enter the MBA program at Harvard
Business School in the fall of 1939. Two years later, he
married Virginia Carnes and took a job with the Republic
Iron and Steel Company, where he worked until joining
the Navy in 1943, seeing perilous action in the North
Atlantic.

Before the war was over, Paul and Jinny had two

children, Williams's and Flossie's first grandchildren, Paul, Jr. (carrying on a precious family name into the next generation) and Suzanne. The new family settled in Rutherford. Paul took a job with Abraham and Straus department store in Brooklyn. It was a long commute every day for thirty years, but his roots in his home town were strong and enduring. Paul rose to become Vice-President in Charge of Operations at A&S.

Quiet and reserved William Eric, meanwhile, was following closely in his father's footsteps, as older children so often do, when his medical training was interrupted by the war. He entered the service as a Navy medical officer on the Pacific front, in February, 1942.

"Is it not a crime," Williams complained bitterly to Robert McAlmon, "for older men to send armies of the young to kill each other for 'countries' or 'principles' or even 'freedom?' "

Williams was helpless to control the large and tragic events that led to this sorry state of affairs. His sons were literally on opposite sides of the world from each other, and mail took weeks to arrive. Williams had more time to reflect about the kind of father he had been, and perhaps believed he should have been. "A father follows the course of his son's life," he wrote young Bill, thousands of miles distant, "and notes things of which he has not the privilege to speak." Twenty years earlier, he found it easier to mend fences with Flossie when she remained far behind in Geneva and he returned to the States for a year. He was also able to communicate more freely with his boys while they were away from home. As a writer, he might have been more comfortable with words on paper than face to face.

Young Bill, involved with his own efforts at writing poetry, for the first time had the courage to ask his dad to send along some poems. He felt mature enough, ready to read and understand his father's literary work, his mysterious side.

Williams was grateful for his son's gesture; nevertheless, he could not help reminiscing. And he asked Bill for forgiveness. One incident in particular stuck stubbornly in Williams's mind, so much so that he mentioned it several times in wartime letters to Bill. It was a day at the end of summer camp season, years and years ago. Bill was in a canoe race, nearing the finish line, heading for certain victory, when another boy cut him off at the last moment. Williams, watching from shore, laughed. His son cried with disappointment, turned upon his father, and said, "It was my only chance to win anything!" Those words came back to haunt Williams and forced him to wonder about other times when he might have done or said the wrong thing.

Bill took pains to shrug off his father's agonies over roads not taken and words unspoken and welcomed his confidences, especially in medical matters. At last, Williams was able to share his accounts of the trials and tribulations of family practice in Rutherford. His son Bill *understood*, man to man, colleague to colleague. And he also heard the barely-hidden message beneath his father's hurried anecdotes about mothers and babies, the babies Williams had ushered into the world twenty years ago and more. For now they were grown women bearing their own children. It was becoming clearer who would care for this new generation of local families, who would be the most likely successor to William Carlos Williams's medical practice. He yearned to cast off the physician's white coat and stethoscope. When office hours extended far into the night, Williams dreamed of giving up his job, to slip away,

> and join
> the old men I once saw
> on the wharf at Villefranche
> fishing for sea-snails,
> with a split stick,
> in the shallow water—

But a vacation was out of the question for Williams and Flossie. Aside from case work; a stalled epic poem

waiting to get written; and correspondence with the boys
(he made it a point to respond to their letters the very
same day they arrived); the aging roof of Nine Ridge Road
badly needed repair. Without a thought for his safety,
Williams climbed up and patched it himself.

Between patients—if Williams was not busy scribbling
notes for a new poem onto prescription pads, or pecking
out a few more lines on the typewriter hidden inside the
fliptop desk in his consulting room—he could often be
found in back of the house. There was always plenty to do
in the garden, weeds to be yanked up between flower beds,
holes to be dug for tulip bulbs. Williams blended rich
compost into the soil, turning it over; or prepared to plant
the sapling brought back from a weekend trip to James
Laughlin's country place in Norfolk, Connecticut, or
Flossie's parents' farm near Harriman, New York. Rooting
around in the dark earth was great exercise. Williams carefully removed his white shirt and tie, and when he had
worked long enough so that sweat began to show through
his undershirt, it never failed, his mind was wonderfully
cleared. He washed up, had a bite to eat, and was ready for
the next visitor.

꿩

On May 2, 1945, the law finally caught up with Ezra
Pound. Under arrest, he was taken to the United States
Army Detention Training Center, a few miles north of
Pisa, on the road to Viareggio, in Italy. He was locked into
an outdoor, six-by-six-and-a-half foot wire mesh cage with
a cement floor and a tar paper roof and two blankets for
a bed. His shoelaces and belt were taken away, and he
was given a loose-fitting army fatigue uniform to wear.
He was not allowed to exercise. Soldiers guarding Pound
were under strict orders not to speak to him. A searchlight
shone down upon him day and night.

Pound worked on his *Cantos* six hours a day, punching

away at the typewriter and humming in a loud voice.
What else was there to do but write? He watched the sun
rise beyond the barbed wire of the camp walls, creating
patterns of light and dark in clouds settling upon the mountain range to the east. He cherished faded memories of
happier days in London, all those decades ago, when he
had been a carefree young man with a red beard. Pound
hoped the constant hard work on his poetry would keep
his mind steady. ". . . And there was a smell of mint under
the tent flaps," he wrote,

> *especially after the rain*
> > *and a white ox on the road toward Pisa*
> > *as if facing the tower,*
> *dark sheep in the drill field and on wet days were clouds*
> *in the mountain as if under the guard roosts*

After three weeks in such harsh conditions, the sixty-year-
old poet was exhausted and near hysteria.

In November, 1945, Pound was flown back to Washington to face nineteen counts of treason involving statements made on his broadcasts. But after being examined
by psychiatrists, early in 1946, he was found insane and
unfit to stand trial. And so, as Prisoner Number 58,102,
he was confined to the imposing, government-run, red
brick St. Elizabeths Mental Hospital overlooking the city
of Washington, DC, where he would spend the next twelve
years.

William Carlos Williams had high standards for *Paterson*
—perhaps too high. It was supposed to unlock the "green
myth" which fascinated him his whole life, the mysterious
natural force behind an industrial, polluted world. It was
supposed to be a poem that showed modern man where he
had gone astray, a poem speaking the truth every new

generation needed to express about a place, through that true way of speaking revealing great beauty. "You can't lie and be a first rate artist," Williams insisted, especially an artist who wanted to paint with words, on one giant canvas, a city to represent all cities.

Paterson would be so focused, in fact, that everything taking place within the poem would happen or be spoken within a few miles of the Passaic River. In its wandering course to the sea, the Passaic stood for the path of Williams's life.

A modern epic, *Paterson* would resemble the great epic works of the past, *The Odyssey, Beowulf, The Song of Roland*. Like them, it would present a noble person in action, Dr. Paterson, alias "Noah Faitoute" (Do-all), alias William Carlos Williams. Like them, it would teach its readers something new about the difficulty of leading a heroic life in times of strife and confusion.

Demanding goals, indeed, for a busy doctor in his sixties, during wartime, his sons gone, and his best and oldest friend locked up for speaking his mind dangerously and at the wrong time. *Paterson* was "the impossible poem," and Williams was distracted away from it. Whenever the radio came on with news of the war overseas, he looked anxiously up from his manuscript. Pulled away from the close, local scene, his thoughts turned to distant lands. Friends like Louis Zukofsky and James Laughlin told him he was trying to put too much into *Paterson*. It grew and grew, and still had no shape. Such comments and criticisms made Williams even more angry with himself, moody, and overwrought.

Undaunted, he went back to Paterson on weekend field trips time and again. He soaked up its atmosphere to the bursting point, filling notebook after notebook with bits and pieces, gossip overheard in bars, at factories, at the silk mills; excerpts from history books and letters; his own philosophies. All this information would have to add up to a definition of the mystery of Paterson the place, and therefore reveal *Paterson* the poem:

APPROACH TO A CITY

Getting through with the world—
I never tire of the mystery
of these streets: the three baskets
of dried flowers in the high

bar-room window, the gulls wheeling
above the factory, the dirty
snow—the humility of the snow that
silvers everything and is

trampled and lined with use—yet
falls again, the silent birds
on the still wires of the sky, the blur
of wings as they take off

together. The flags in the heavy
air move against a leaden
ground—the snow
pencilled with the stubble of old

weeds: I never tire of these sights
but refresh myself there
always for there is small holiness
to be found in braver things.

The inspiring rush of the Great Falls—like the soothing rush of water near Williams's ear at Gratwick Highlands, the rush of the sea past the ocean liner carrying him home from France, the rush of the Hudson River past the ferry taking him into the city as a schoolboy—gave Williams the strength to go on with *Paterson*. The roaring falls spoke to him of nature's power at the center of an industrial city, of hope for nature's survival, and of his own enduring faith in poetry. He had no choice but to believe in the falls and what they stood for, and he gave them center stage in *Book I* of *Paterson*:

> *Jostled as are the waters approaching*
> *the brink, his thoughts*
> *interlace, repel, and cut under*

Williams had no choice but to see a reminder of himself, the solitary poet, in the single branch of a lonely tree holding on for dear life at the brink of the Great Falls:

> *—and watch, wrapt! one branch*
> *of the tree at the fall's edge, one*
> *mottled branch, withheld,*
> *among the gyrate branches*
> *of the waist-thick sycamore,*
> *sway less, among the rest, separate, slowly*

He pushed himself hard. When the proof sheets for *Book I* arrived, he covered them with so many corrections and revisions he could hardly see the words. Publication date was set for July, 1946. In May of that year, Williams underwent a hernia operation, repeated again in December.

The war over, Bill and Paul safely home again, and the poem *Paterson* miraculously begun, Williams's tired body was telling him it was time to breathe a little easier and slow down.

But he did not seem to hear it.

XI

"The descent beckons
as the ascent beckoned"

It was a fine day in October, 1947. Ezra Pound, a shawl draped across his shoulders, slouched in a lounge chair, tossing peanuts to a growing crowd of hungry squirrels and chirping bluejays. He never stopped moving. His long fingers twitched restlessly, and he pressed one shoulder, then the other, into the canvas behind his back. Off to the side, his wife, Dorothy, sat and waited.

A familiar, athletic figure approached, making his way across the sweeping lawn of the mental hospital. It was a sprightly, well-dressed man, walking, as he always did, slightly pigeon-toed, arms swinging loosely at his sides. His big brown eyes seemed even larger behind thick-lensed glasses.

At long last, William Carlos Williams had found the courage to make a first visit to his old friend at St. Elizabeths. More than a year before, he wrote apologetically to Pound, "I feel ashamed when I lose my temper over you . . . It's a shabby business, you in an asylum and I much too occupied with my own affairs, to carry on this way—like two children." Today, Williams was nervous. The hos-

pital's barred windows and stone walls loomed darkly at
the top of the hill. It was a cold fortress of a place.

Pound's beard was still scruffy, his smile still puzzling
(was he laughing *with* you, or *at* you?), his laugh like a
coarse cough. His handshake, though, was eager, strong,
and welcoming.

Pound spoke bitterly of his wartime broadcasts, insisted once again they were not intended to be treasonous.
He was only trying to save the Constitution of the United
States from ruin. Three psychiatrists found him to be of
unsound mind because he dared speak out? So be it! A man
had to take *some* risks for the sake of his opinions!

Avoiding Williams's gaze, Pound pressed his finger-
tips tensely to his forehead and looked away, jumping,
like the bluejays at his feet, to another subject. Had Williams begun to read the books he recommended in his last
letter? When was he going to accept the importance of
scholarship? Since student days they had been arguing,
about the writer's responsibility to know all the literature
that had come before. Pound bawled out his sensitive
friend, the country doctor who would never understand.

Williams's visits to see Pound made him tired. Ezra
held back so much, had an annoying way of throwing people off guard. He simply would not reply to personal questions. All he wanted to talk about was what was on *his*
mind at the time. Williams was frustrated: "*Never explain
anything*, that was Pound's motto." As a matter of fact,
Ezra was and always had been a spoiled brat who had to
have his way.

Williams came away from his occasional audiences
with "The Great Man" feeling a little bit jealous, too.
Confinement gave Pound unlimited time to write. In the
years at St. Elizabeths, he came out with three new books
—new *Cantos*, translations from Confucius and Sophocles
—as well as more than one hundred articles for magazines and journals. Pound had endless time to read, too,
twenty-five books devoured in a good week, provided by

friends, and by the willing staff at the Library of Congress nearby.

Pound's cell, its large window facing the Capitol Building, was at the back of the second floor of St. Elizabeth's, at the top of a spiral staircase. It was a messy room, with pieces of paper, envelopes, books, pens and pencils, cardboard files, old paint cans, and dishes filled with scraps of food lying on the floor. Pound carried on with his work there and served visitors tea in peanut butter jars.

All in all, life could have been worse. Pound was never asked to help with housekeeping duties around the ward, nor was he required to have psychiatric treatment. And William Carlos Williams was not his only visitor. Pound received a stream of other friends and admirers, most of the literary lights of the day: Archibald MacLeish, T. S. Eliot, E. E. Cummings, Robert Lowell, Charles Olson, Thornton Wilder, and Marianne Moore.

Despite Ezra Pound's irritating manner, Williams continued to admire him and could not deny the man's talent as a poet and writer; quite simply, he was the best of their generation. He led the way, a champion of the American language. The two men would always have this common ideal. It shone over all their poetic and political differences.

Ezra Pound led a life in total devotion to literature, with nothing else to think about from dawn to dusk except expressing his ideas. Surely you did not have to be locked up to enjoy that privilege. From time to time throughout his decades as a physician, Williams had flashes of a new life after medicine. Now, he dreamed more and more—as he neared sixty-five—of a "longed-for time" when, like Pound, he, too, would "be able to hobnob with my few rare friends more than I wish to." He dreamed of becoming a gardener, imagined moving upstate, hiring himself on as a groundskeeper for the Abbotts and the Gratwicks. What could be finer? Mornings at the typewriter, a break to plant and weed the garden, then back to writing, and so on leisurely through the day.

Young Bill Williams would soon be finishing his training at New York Hospital, across the river on Manhattan's East Side, and there was no doubt in his father's mind, his son was the perfect person to fill his shoes. The practice Williams had built up over forty years would pass on smoothly. And father and son shared the same philosophy about fees. The Williams doctors were not out to take advantage of the poor people who came to them. That was unheard of at Nine Ridge Road. They got by, without worrying all that much about money.

> *Being in this stage*
> *I look to the last,*
> *see myself returning:*
> *the seamed face*
> *as of a tired rider*
> *upon a tired horse*
> *coming up*

A sudden heart attack in February, 1948, darkened William Carlos Williams's fantasy of freedom.

Lying in a hospital bed, he began to scribble furiously in his red pocket-sized notebook. First sketches for chapters of his *Autobiography* took quick shape. If death came, he wanted to leave behind a memoir of his life and times. During six weeks of recuperation, Williams delved deep in his memory and discovered to his delight how easily recollections of youth came back. He was not too concerned with accuracy. He wanted impressions—as if opening up a dusty family photograph album long abandoned in the attic. Snapshots of childhood and youth awaited.

He also made a forthright and at the same time self-protecting statement on the very first page of the book: "I do not intend to tell the particulars of the women I have been to bed with, or anything about them," Williams warned his curious readers in advance, "I am extremely sexual in my desires," he went on, but "the manner in which [I directed] that power" is "secret . . . The hidden core of my life will not easily be deciphered."

Before Williams left the hospital, he managed to outline eleven chapters of the book. He began, naturally, at the beginning: early years in peaceful, small-town Rutherford. Then, at Penn, the endless struggle began, which never ceased to move him—between medicine and poetry, rounding out William Carlos Williams's full and frantic life.

Over the summer of 1948, Nine Ridge Road was a scene of sawdust, noise, and milling workmen, as a new, expanded pediatrics office wing took shape in anticipation of young Bill's arrival. Williams's colleagues at Passaic General Hospital, where he served as Head of Pediatrics and President of the Medical Board, and where he had been on staff for more than twenty years, gave him an electric typewriter as a parting gift when he retired that fall. Of course, Williams could not refuse such a generous gesture, but he confided to Flossie how much he disliked the machine. Why, half the pleasure of writing was to *bang* out the pages, hunt and peck style, to pound away and get all his pent-up energy out into the open.

It would be another two years before Williams retired completely from medical practice, but with his departure from Passaic General, and dutiful son William Eric's phasing-in, a gradual withdrawal began. To his surprise, but not unexpectedly to close friends who knew him well, newfound time did not rest all that easily upon Williams. It was hard to let go of a profession that had been, as he liked to say, his "very food and drink . . . Every sort of individual that is possible to imagine in some phase of his development, from the highest to the lowest, at some time exhibited himself" to Doc Williams.

His short poem, "To Close," spoke of Williams's bittersweet feelings as he began to sense medical life receding:

> *Will you please rush down and see*
> *ma baby. You know, the one I talked*
> *to you about last night*
>
> *What was that?*
>
> *Is this the baby specialist?*
>
> *Yes, but perhaps you mean my son,*
> *can't you wait until . ?*
>
> *I, I, I don't think it's brEAthin'*

Too much idleness was even more painful than the excess nervous activity which led to Williams's heart attack. It was time to get on the lecture circuit, the best cure of all. In the late 1940s and early '50s, Williams took it upon himself to become a spokesman for "the new poetry" from his point of view as elder statesman. Invitations came, from far and wide, many in response to the impressive debut of *Paterson.* Flossie accompanied her husband often, to provide support; his health was not quite what it used to be. Close to home, Rutgers, NYU, Bard College, Cooper Union, the New School, Yale, and Vassar asked Williams to speak. Farther afield, Harvard, Dartmouth, Bennington College, the University of Buffalo, the University of Oregon, Reed College, the University of Washington, and UCLA beckoned.

Williams believed young people held the future of American letters in their hearts and minds, and he openly preached to them. "Take the oyster," he told a group of Rutherford High School students, "A grain of sand enters its secret domain, in other words, between its shells. The poor oyster . . . frets over it, rolling it back and forth, until, miracle of miracles, it makes of it a beautiful thing, a pearl! That is the artist at work."

He was fond of destroying the illusions of his student audiences about the kind of environment a writer needed in order to create. It did not make any difference to Williams *where* he was; he could always write. In his own home, he revealed, he had three different writing tables: one to sit at, naturally; one to stand up to, the way Ernest Hemingway liked to do it; and one beside his bed, if inspiration should hit him like a flash—as it so often did—in the middle of the night.

"Why does every line of a poem *have* to begin with a capital letter?" he challenged the young people, "It's annoying . . . We don't *speak* in iambic pentameter . . . Our language is free! It is the language that we *hear* which should go into a poem."

He told them to use the language of the street and of their homes in their poetry, to write of matters in everyday life that concerned them, to look and listen carefully to the world around them, first of all and always, for, "What is poetry, anyhow—but the *music* of words?"

He held up his own life path as a model for the students. Had not he, Dr. Williams, chosen a career, as well as a life in the arts, and had he not found a way—hectic and frustrating at times, to be sure—to make this double life work as one? It took the courage of his convictions, a healthy dose of idealism, and belief in a cause: to save the American language by writing about American experience in a plain, no-nonsense, poetic way.

"But this language of yours," asked one of the English instructors at a reception after a rousing poetry reading and discussion, "Where does it come from?"

"From the mouths of Polish mothers," Williams replied sharply, thinking of the Passaic housewives who opened their homes to him so he might heal their children, and also allowed him to experience, freshly, day by day, the unique, melting-pot character that flavored American society.

In his speeches, Williams also reflected back to his first influences in poetry, reciting more and more often from Walt Whitman, who had been, with Keats, an early idol all those years ago, when he was the same age as the young people he addressed. Whitman was still an important force, a proud example of bravery in poetry, because he made use of the native American language, *not* English, and he said exactly what he meant, always in an emotional style.

Williams was invited to address a conference in Salt Lake City, Utah, and wanted to drive there, a six-day trip cross-country. Flossie, unfortunately, had never learned to drive, so she could not help out—but sister Lottie was happy to. She was visiting from Los Angeles, where— except for a stint during World War II, when she took an apartment in New York City—she had lived with her younger son, Eyvind, since her marriage broke up in 1925. He was now an artist with Walt Disney Studios, having inherited his father's skill with a paintbrush.

Williams read to the Salt Lake City audience from his favorite Whitman poem, "Song of Myself," and also from a recent discovery, close to his present cause, "Respondez!"

> *Let every one answer! let those who sleep be waked!*
> > *let none evade!*
> *Must we still go on with our affections and sneaking?*
> *Let me bring this to a close—I pronounce openly*
> > *for a new distribution of roles;*
> *Let that which stood in front go behind; and let that*
> > *which was behind advance to the front and speak*

"The first thing to do in hearing poems," William Carlos Williams advised a packed, reverently hushed roomful of college undergraduates at UCLA, "is not to try to understand them at the start at least, but to *listen* . . . Let the poem come to you . . . Put all you have into trying to *hear* the poem . . . Later, perhaps, you may discover what it means."

So many young readers of poetry were mystified right away, because they tried too hard to make sense out of a poem, assuming it must be taken as a puzzle, or a riddle, to be solved. Williams told the creative writing students at UCLA and elsewhere to allow the poem's tones and harmonies to enter their imaginations first, paving the way for a message.

From Los Angeles, Williams and Flossie took the train to Taos, New Mexico, to visit their old and dear friend from *Contact* magazine and Paris days, Robert McAlmon. Williams worked hard to capture and convey the music of the event in a new poem. He was experimenting with shape, letting the lines reach out farther across the page. Once more, memory revealed itself to the aging poet:

> *Leaving California to return east, the fertile desert,*
> *(were it to get water)*
> *surrounded us, a music of survival, subdued, distant, half*
> *heard; we were engulfed*
> *by it as in the early evening, seeing the wind lift*
> *and drive the sand, we*
> *passed Yuma. All night long, heading for El Paso to*
> *meet our friend,*
> *we slept fitfully. Thinking of Paris, I waked to the tick*
> *of the rails. The*
> *jagged desert*

৵৽

William Carlos Williams's mother, his stern, cantankerous, beloved Elena, was dying. She had been moved out of her upstairs quarters at Nine Ridge Road, and was being cared for by an elderly English couple in town. They made sure she ate her favorite foods and even allowed her an occa-

sional nip of sherry. Williams, always the attentive son,
continued to visit her every day. But as winter gave way
to spring in 1949, it was clear to his medically-trained eye
that the end was near. She failed to recognize her son,
shocked him by deliriously screaming at him as if he were
an intruder. She scolded him for not respecting her enough,
even as Williams knew full well he had never been more
than a few minutes away. Her sight was gone. Her memory
played tricks on her.

She died in her sleep, on October 7th, 1949, at the age
of 102. "Come back, Mother, come back from/the dead—"
Williams called to Raquel Helene, out of his grief,

> *Where I cannot yet join you . . .*
> *It is the loveless soul, the soul*
> *of things that has surpassed*
> *our loves. In this—you live,*
> *Mother, live in me   .*
>   *always*

After a childhood spent in the tropics, Mrs. Williams
never completely adjusted to life in Rutherford. She had
never been truly happy in America. She kept herself separate from other women in town. As she slipped away from
life, Williams saw her slipping away from him, too. He
feared her going. Over the thirty years since her husband's
death, Raquel Helene became more and more a companion
to her son. He kept a record of her youthful reminiscences
and homespun proverbs, hoping to prolong her life, secretly
imagining she might even outlive him.

Soon after the funeral, rummaging through his
mother's things in a huge steamer trunk in the attic, Williams came across a box with three gold medals Raquel
Helene had won for her painting and drawing when she
was an art student in Paris in the late 1870s. In all the
hours Williams had spent sitting by her sickbed and chat-
ting with her, whiling away the afternoons, she never told

him about those long-ago successes. He was angry and became even more so when he discovered her Mass Book from the days when she had been a practicing Catholic. Folded inside was a letter, dated 1880, from a certain Mr. De Longueville, proposing marriage. Why, that was before she met William George Williams! Another secret withheld, from the doctor who prided himself on being able to tell what ailed a patient after an intensive half hour's examination, the doctor who believed the unexplored land of man's mind and body was the rightful province of the knowing physician. Why had his mother kept such important secrets from him? He would never, never know.

Five weeks later, young Bill Williams married Daphne Spence and settled down to live and work in Rutherford. At one time he had given some thought to moving to the Pacific Northwest, a part of the country he fell in love with as a young man. But, like brother Paul, his roots in Rutherford were strong; besides, his dad was counting on him. Young Bill was well on his way to a flourishing practice in family medicine.

The following September, 1950, Bill and Daphne's first daughter (they would have three more girls) was born. They named her Emily, after William Carlos Williams's English grandmother.

Williams was shaken by his mother's passing. But the work needed to go on. By 1950, Books I, II, and III of *Paterson* were published. He took a splendid opportunity to delve more deeply into Book IV, when he spent the summer as a guest of honor at Yaddo, an artists' colony in Saratoga Springs, New York. The daily routine there was strict, allowing no socializing until dinner hour. Yaddo was a place for one pursuit and one only, creativity. Each artist, writer, and composer had his or her private studio. Williams's room, the most glamorous of all, was on the

top floor of the estate's magnificent main building, overlooking a wide expanse of pasture and a carefully tended
rose garden.

Williams noticed that poets who had spent time in the
room in past years had etched their names into the glass
windowpane. The grandeur and tradition of his tower room
were too much for him. He moved into a more appropriate
humble log cabin deep in the forest, with a wood-burning
fireplace to take the chill off misty summer nights. There,
Williams thrived in the free and quiet atmosphere, and, far
from homebound worries, worked smoothly and with pleasure on *Paterson IV*.

Paterson, an industrial metropolis, had its beginnings, as did the rest of America, in what Williams believed were purer, more natural times. In the eighteenth
century, when only the Totowa Indian tribe inhabited the
neighboring countryside, Paterson, like Rutherford, was
little more than a village hidden by thick foliage. There
were perhaps ten farm houses where, in a hundred years,
Paterson the city would spring up. In *Book IV*, Williams
painted a memory-picture of those good old days:

> *The sun goes behind Garrett Mountain*
> *as evening descends, the green of its pine*
> *trees, fading under a crimson sky until*
> *all color is lost. In the town candle light*
> *appears. No lighted streets*

The difficulties of *Book I* were far behind him.

Besides the exciting invitations to visit colleges, and the
productive stay at Yaddo, awards and honors finally began
to come Williams's way. In 1948, he received the Russell
Loines Award from the National Institute of Arts and
Letters. The one thousand dollar prize accompanying the
medal was welcome. But more important was Williams's

thrill at being introduced to the audience at the ceremony by his old friend, Marianne Moore.

Honorary degrees came from the University of Buffalo, Bard College, and Rutgers. He was declared Poet Laureate of New Jersey. In 1950, Williams received the coveted National Book Award's Gold Medal for Poetry, in recognition of *Paterson III* and his *Selected Poems. Time* magazine, and the *New York Times Book Review* wrote feature stories about the high-spirited doctor-poet from Rutherford.

&

Like the renowned, massive iron engines at the Paterson Locomotive Works, Williams, building up a head of steam, charged down the tracks into his seventh decade with new vigor—until a stroke in March, 1951, knocked him down.

His vision blurred, his senses drowned in numbness, his mood sank. When he turned to the white page, he found only a tortured world awaiting him. A cruel kind of memory would not let him sleep. His body stilled. His mind took control and seemed to play games with him. The mind was, he confessed in a poem dedicated to his two daughters-in-law, Daphne and Virginia, "the cause of our distresses . . . And I am not/a young man./My love encumbers me . . ."

To friends Eleanora and Bill Monahan, he wrote, in another lonely and melancholy mood:

> *in the winter of the year,*
> *the birds who know how*
> *to escape suffering*
> *by flight*
> *are gone. Man alone*
> *is that creature who*
> *cannot escape suffering*
> *by flight*

Early in 1952, Williams was asked by librarian Luther Evans if he would like to serve as Consultant in Poetry at the Library of Congress in Washington. It was a great honor, requiring little responsibility except for ceremonial readings and receptions. The term was to begin in September.

But a second stroke descended viciously in August, 1952, while Williams and Floss were on vacation at Gratwick Highlands. It was a staggering blow. Williams lost the use of the upper right side of his body, and, terrifyingly, his powers of speech and vision, which only slowly and with difficulty returned. Grudgingly, the electric typewriter was pulled into service. He tried to continue writing by searching around the keyboard with the forefinger of his left hand, letter by letter by letter. But he could not think straight. It was as if the upper half of his brain were wrapped in cotton.

The Library of Congress position was put off until December, by which time Williams prayed he would be well enough to serve. A listless depression muddled his thoughts. He wandered around his empty house like a crippled beast, short-tempered and footloose.

As the months wore on and the year waned, Williams lost hope of ever going to Washington. He was under investigation by the Library, suspected of being a Communist sympathizer. His old associations with Ezra Pound and a few antiwar petitions he once signed came back to haunt him, made much more serious than they actually were because of the anti-Communist climate seizing the country.

Williams hired a lawyer to negotiate for him with the Library. That move did not go over well. In January, 1953, his appointment was taken away, supposedly because of Williams's continuing ill health, and the library's doubts about whether he would be up to the task of working there. Even though the appointment was then reinstated as of May 15, the term was scheduled to end in June, anyway.

Williams wondered how many successes and failures,

endless ups and downs, a man could take in his lifetime. Who was left to help him now? Ezra Pound was beyond reach in an asylum. Bob McAlmon, out West, was a sickly shadow of his former self. Williams's two boys were involved with their new wives and growing families. His mother and father were gone.

Faithful, devoted Flossie was still by his side. But heavy and painful secrets kept from her over four decades of marriage remained to be revealed. Would he ever be able to face such a moment? Would he ever have the strength to confront his wife and show her his *true* self?

❦

Words took vague, nervous shape in William Carlos Williams's brain. Then, just as he was about to speak, they slipped away, like butterflies, lovely, light, airy—gone. He started anew, tried to explain how he felt to his friend Kenneth Burke. Surely he could understand that frustrated feeling; they had known each other for thirty years now.

Williams, speechless, in despair of speech, grasped the air between his cupped, outstretched hands, facing each other at chest level, then, trembling, drew his hands toward him and downward in a curve, as he groped to describe what he now missed, the practiced motion of an obstetrician delivering a baby. Williams's pleading eyes met his philosopher friend's sharp and sympathetic gaze.

"Yes, I do understand," Burke thought, ruefully. "The strokes have cut into Bill's life-rhythm. He has lost his quick, clear, upbeat charm. He has lost all ability to be spontaneous. That is the root of his suffering, and there is nothing I can do about it."

Williams felt like the tall weeds he had glimpsed countless times when he drove past the railroad embankment in years past. The weeds held on to the cinder-strewn ground for all they were worth, buffeted this way and that at the wind's whim. There was a war waging in his saddened brain. His eyes jumped out of focus, suddenly, without warning. He was no longer certain which force was winning: his imagination, or a gnawing fear of death.

In February, 1953, his sadness and depression became too heavy to bear. He was admitted to Hillside Hospital in Floral Park, Queens.

ॐ

"I love the locust tree," Williams wrote in *Paterson III*,

>   *the sweet white locust*
>   *How much?*
>   *How much?*
>   *How much does it cost*
>   *to love the locust tree*
>   *in bloom?*

In his therapy sessions at Hillside, Williams struggled with this very question. What *had* been the cost to family and friends—how much damage had been done to his home life—because he was consumed by single-minded dedication to poetry, to the endless, romantic pursuit of beauty in nature? His sons denied Williams's guilty idea of himself as a neglectful father. Bill and Paul insisted he had *always* been there when they needed him. They harbored no resentful feelings, no painful memories of a father ignoring them, preferring to be in New York City on a weekend with literary friends, instead of tossing a baseball around in the back yard with his boys. Was Williams painting a false portrait of himself in old age? Was he no longer able to see the past in clear focus?

He was guilty about being a poet. He wondered whether his poems were any good at all. He could not tell anymore. Would his work stand the test of time? Would it endure, alongside the poetry of Pound, Marianne Moore, H.D., T. S. Eliot and Wallace Stevens—or would William

Carlos Williams die unknown to the next generation, despite all the traveling and preaching he had done?

At Hillside, he was allowed one phone call per week. He was not permitted to have a typewriter, and so he wrote, every single day, shakily, by hand, to Flossie. He confessed openly to her that he had failed her. More than the crazy pace of his life had led him to this hospital. More than fears about his possible false steps as a poet and father possessed him.

He was overcome with guilt about his false steps as a husband. Reciting names, dates, and places to Flossie, he told his wife he had been with many other women during their forty married years. He could not help himself. Women—all women—fascinated Williams, beyond words.

Flossie was always a quieter person than her husband, known to speak her mind only when the occasion warranted. She kept her thoughts to herself, concentrated upon running the household and looking after the boys and their families, too. That was a job in itself, and she did it supremely well. She fought down her occasional impulses to keep Williams within bounds, because she respected the delicate part of him, the part that made poems.

Of course, at times she suspected him of infidelity. To what extent? How did she react? This is still not known, because Flossie was such a private woman to the end. She always believed in the strong and sacred bond of marriage. She loved her husband.

Williams had taken advantage of Flossie's quietness and faith, turning to other women, in New York City and elsewhere. He thought back to many nights when he came home at three in the morning, first from a housecall, then a secret rendezvous, only to seek further refuge at his typewriter, while Flossie lay in bed, alone once again. How she must have suffered!

"Having your love/I was rich," Williams wrote to his wife, "Thinking to have lost it/I am tortured/and cannot rest." Now he begged her, his Flossie, his flower, to forgive his unfaithfulness.

XII

"Heel & toe to the end"

> *In old age*
> > *the mind*
> > > > *casts off*
> > > *rebelliously*
> > *an eagle*
> *from its crag*

How many times over four decades as a doctor, how many mornings sitting, waiting at the bedside of a woman in labor, had he watched dawn come, and with it, a new baby's cries?

And now, in the spring of his seventieth year, freed from the asylum but facing the idea of death, William Carlos Williams, troubled and sleepless, sat at the desk in his second floor study, waiting once more, this time for dawn to bring him the birth of a poem. The only sounds in the half-darkness, half-light were the faint hum of the electric typewriter, and indistinct bird rustlings among bushes in the garden below. He waited, tried to stir and rouse his stubborn imagination to action. Tap . . . tap . . . tap . . . laboriously, ever-so-slowly, his limp right hand, guided at the wrist by his strong left hand, hovered uncertainly over a once-familiar keyboard, now a fogged-

over blur of letters. Like a hummingbird, his forefinger
descended here, and there, seeking out one letter, then the
next. Each letter spelled life, life, life. Each pause—recog-
nizing the deep silence between words—spelled death.
Each letter struck spelled survival, one more step deeper
into action and energy, as Williams performed the restless
act above all else keeping him alive.

Christopher Columbus, Williams's hero to the end,
was a man who did not retreat. He embarked upon a voyage of discovery to beat back the darkness. Columbus kept
going; he had no choice. Perhaps some final fury lay beyond the horizon, in a land no one had ever seen—but the
chance cried out for the taking. And Williams's poems
cried out for the writing, no matter how many wrong keys
were struck, no matter how many times the poet ripped
error-strewn sheets of yellow paper from the typewriter,
the carriage squealing in protest, no matter how many
tightly balled scraps of paper ended up piled randomly
in the corner of the room. Like Columbus, Williams pushed
on, against the dying of the light.

Where did such desperate energy come from? Williams did not stop to think about it. There wasn't time.
The demon in his mind drove the poet onward, "approach-
ing/death . . . possessed by many poems."

Faith in the turning year, the seasons always before
him, heralded by his dependable friends the flowers, helped
Williams face the future:

>*This is the time*
>*for which we have been*
>*waiting*

>*cherry blossom time*
>*when lilacs are in bloom*

There was a time, not long before, when he took refuge
in his garden from a bustling life. Wearied now by an hour

of writing, Williams hobbled past Flossie's beloved rose bushes; they would be next to come forth in blossom.

The garden was a place of renewal closest to home. Although his eagle-mind sometimes danced and flew among the clouds, Williams's tired body was taking root, slowly turning back to the earth.

❧

And so, the young people came to Rutherford to pay homage to the old man.

Twenty-seven-year-old fledgling poet and teacher Robert Creeley—accompanied by Cynthia Homire, a friend from Black Mountain College—stood on the front steps of Nine Ridge Road one afternoon in early spring, 1954, rang the doorbell, and waited, trembling, to meet his idol for the first time.

An admirer of Williams for ten years, Robert Creeley grew up in Arlington, Massachusetts. His father, also a doctor, died when Robert was four years old. His mother, a nurse, raised him humbly and modestly. When he first became interested in poetry while at the Holderness School in Plymouth, New Hampshire, Robert turned to the work of William Carlos Williams because he had come to favor the simple, direct, common-talk way his poems expressed feelings the boy could understand. He read the *Complete Collected Poems*, and *The Wedge*. These books made a lasting impression. When Creeley and another young friend, Bob Leed, founded a little magazine, *The Lititz Review*, they took courage and wrote to their heroes, Pound and Williams, requesting new poems to publish. Williams responded warmly and generously with poetry, and, of course, advice.

The door opened. There stood William Carlos Williams himself: a compact, stooped over, wiry gentleman of medium height; eyes gleaming, kind, and straightforward behind glasses; hair quite white, thinning, combed straight back; dressed neatly and comfortably, shoes well-

polished, trousers sharply creased. Creeley's first thought
was, "He reminds me of the first time I saw Pablo Picasso,
in a café in Aix-en-Provence! The same energy in his
presence . . . the same vitality in an old man . . ." Creeley
paled. He opened his mouth, but no words came.

"What's the matter?" asked Dr. Williams with a
smile, extending a well-scrubbed hand in greeting, already
forming the correct diagnosis in his mind.

"I . . . I've never been so scared in my life!" Robert
Creeley managed to reply.

Williams laughed delightedly, and beckoned the two
visitors in. Flossie emerged with drinks. Soon, everyone
felt at home. "Would you like to see my study?" Williams
asked. He guided Creeley up the narrow stairs, dragging
his right foot slightly as he climbed.

Williams took the young man's elbow and guided him
to a window overlooking the garden. "You see the garage
back there?" he said, pointing to the low building at the
end of a thirty-foot stone walk made up of fieldstones
Williams had collected and laid in himself, "I dream of
reviving our Tyro Theatre group from the twenties and
thirties . . . to start putting on performances there, like we
used to . . . in the old days . . ." He was lost in a memory
and his gaze drifted off, then returned, "You know," Williams whispered, grasping Creeley's arm more tightly, "I
had to tell Flossie about my affairs with other women . . .
I *had* to confess to her . . . I wanted . . . I needed a clean
slate . . . After all she had to put up with," he paused for a
long moment, "I don't know . . . what she must *think* of
me now."

Williams's speech came in short, impulsive bursts. He
halted to search for the right expression, exclaiming loudly,
in frustration, "Oh for God's sake!" when the words did
not keep pace with his enthusiasm. Creeley found it hard
to follow him at times. It was as if Williams's mind were
laid bare, fragments of thought jostling with each other to
be set free.

Stories told about Flossie the renowned hostess and

cook proved true. The dinner was delicious. There was one
uneasy moment, when she asked Creeley to cut Williams's
steak for him. Since the strokes, her husband had trouble
handling a knife and fork. The young man, in his zeal,
sliced pieces tinier than bite-sized. "Hey! I'm not a baby,
you know!" insisted the old poet proudly. At times like
this, when Williams became excited over small matters,
Flossie was quick to hush and calm him. "I do fear for
Bill's health," she told Creeley later, "Sometimes when he
goes to bed for an afternoon nap, I wonder if he'll be up
again."

On the drive back to New York City, Robert Creeley
was pensive and sober. Finally meeting the man, Williams
himself, he learned an important lesson. Unless he took
risks, unless he could convince himself "to go for broke,"
as Williams had always done, nothing would ever come of
his writing or his life. But first, Creeley had to look more
deeply into himself, take an honest look at his capabilities
as a writer, and more significantly as a *person*. Just what,
exactly, did he believe in? What causes were worth the risk
of defending?

Robert Creeley admired Williams because he had
never given up the endless self-searching or the endless
risk-taking required to keep the American language alive
and well.

&

Other young poets and writers traveled to Nine Ridge
Road for a chat, a drink, a tour of the house and garden,
a view from the upstairs window, a pat on the back, an inspiration, an impromptu poetry reading in the living room,
one of Flossie's hearty meals, or just to listen to Williams's
tireless encouragement that they keep on writing, at all
costs. The list of those who visited Williams goes on and
on: David Ignatow, whose first book of poems Williams
praised from the podium at the Ninety-second Street
YMHA in 1948; Allen Ginsberg, born in Newark, who at

twenty-three wrote to a flattered Williams from the city of Paterson, "I know you will be pleased to realize that at least one actual citizen of your community has inherited your experience in his struggle to love and know his own world and city;" English-born Denise Levertov, whom Williams praised more than any other poet of her generation; Cid Corman, Robert Lowell, Babette Deutsch, Galway Kinnell, James Wright, Hyam Plutzik, Theodore Roethke, Jonathan Williams, Gilbert Sorrentino, Joel Oppenheimer, and many others.

If they did not make the pilgrimage to Rutherford, the new generation of poets wrote to William Carlos Williams enclosing manuscripts, asking, would he, could he please take a few minutes to tell them if they were on the right track? What were they doing right in their verse? What were they doing wrong? He answered each and every letter that came to him—usually the very same day.

⋐

"It is winter," Williams wrote to Flossie in his late, long love poem, "Asphodel, That Greeny Flower,"

> *and there*
> > *waiting for you to care for them*
> *are your plants.*
> > *Poor things! you say*
> > > *as you compassionately*
> *pour at their roots*
> > *the reviving water.*
> > > *Lean-cheeked*
> *I say to myself*
> > *kindness moves her*
> > > *shall she not be kind*
> *also to me?*

In old age, William Carlos Williams's love for his wife was reborn. But Flossie's love had never died. Through fifty years of marriage, she never stopped being kind to her husband.

"What power has love but forgiveness?" he wondered plaintively in "Asphodel." Now, more than ever, Williams needed her. Through her constant presence, Flossie forgave him.

When Williams broke into a cold sweat before going up on stage for a poetry reading, Flossie was there, to straighten his tie and whisper a few words into his ear.

When he suffered a stroke, and another, and another, and another; when he was feeble and emaciated at one hundred twenty pounds, recovering from a cancer operation, she was there—always stable, always practical—to nurse him back to health.

When the telephone wouldn't stop ringing, and Williams was too weak to answer it; when the doorbell wouldn't stop ringing, with well-intentioned visitors waiting, Flossie was there, with a sharp, firm voice and a wary smile.

When, of a spring morning, Williams donned his straw hat and seersucker jacket for a leisurely, two-block stroll over to the library or the post office; and, hours later, Flossie got a call from a former patient of her husband's, saying Doc Williams ended up at her house for no apparent reason, dazed and disoriented, Flossie was there to come and get him—and scold him.

When, in a fit of depression, he stepped into the path of an oncoming car in front of the house on Ridge Road and narrowly escaped certain death, she was there— to bawl him out.

When Williams got so excited by a new poem he was working on that he could not sleep; when, during an interview, he became at a loss for words, got stirred up and angry at himself; she was there to complete his unfinished sentences and soothe him.

When, confused, he accidentally tore up and threw into the trash bin the completed manuscript for his last book of poems, *Pictures from Breughel*, she was there to retrieve it, paste the pages back together, and mail it off to James Laughlin at New Directions.

When tears clouded his eyes, and Williams could not see the typewriter keyboard, his last letters became so incoherent they were illegible. Flossie was there, to proofread his correspondence and add brief notes at the bottom of the page.

A passion for Greek literature overcame him, and he simply had to read the *Iliad* and the *Odyssey*, to learn more about other heroes in adversity through the words of Homer, another blind poet; but he could no longer see the printed page. Flossie was there, during long evenings spent in the front parlor, to read to her husband, hour after hour until she grew hoarse and could not continue. She read everything to him, magazines, books, letters, manuscripts, essays, even articles from medical journals. Williams sat on the sofa, his hands clasped tightly between his knees, his head tilted slightly, listening gratefully and intently to the voice of his devoted wife.

For his part, Williams spoke lovingly to Flossie in his poetry. Finally, there could be no other way, no better way for a poet to address his beloved. In "Asphodel," he remembered their wedding day, December 12, 1912, when he "thought the world/stood still,"

> *At the altar*
> *so intent was I*
> *before my vows,*
> *so moved by your presence*
> *a girl so pale*
> *and ready to faint*
> *that I pitied*
> *and wanted to protect you.*
> *As I think of it now,*
> *after a lifetime,*
> *it is as if*
> *a sweet-scented flower*
> *were poised*
> *and for me did open.*

The tide had turned. Williams realized that his Flossie, his once-fragile flower, now pitied and courageously protected *him*.

~ॐ

On April 18, 1958, the indictment of treason against Ezra Pound was dismissed. After a dozen years at St. Elizabeths, he was released to the custody of his wife, Dorothy.

Pound's plans were crystal clear. First, he made a sentimental journey back to the romantic scenes of his youth, his childhood home in Wyncote, Pennsylvania; to the apple tree where he once frolicked with Hilda Doolittle. Late one night, he awoke, slipped out of his house in his pajamas, and walked down to the Presbyterian Church, where he sat in silence on the steps and gazed out over the quiet, sleepy town.

His last stop before returning to Italy at the end of June was, of course, Nine Ridge Road. The final meeting between Ezra Pound and William Carlos Williams was a less than joyful one. They both knew this was the end. A true conversation was impossible. Pound was preoccupied with thoughts of his voyage to Genoa the next day. He took off his shirt and lay down on the couch in the front room expecting to be waited on. Flossie was deeply offended. She had never cared for Ezra very much. As far as she was concerned, it was good riddance.

"If I were a dog," Williams wrote, in his poem, "To My Friend Ezra Pound,"

> *I'd sit down on a cold pavement*
> *in the rain*
> *to wait for a friend (and so would you)*

Over the half-century since graduation from Penn, Williams and Pound had spent no more than a handful of days together, here and there in Rutherford, London, Paris, and

Washington. They inhabited different sides of the world. At the root of their friendship there was always mutual, if grudging respect—from a distance. They were ready and willing to praise each other's work, even if they did not see eye to eye on matters other than literary ones. They both relished a good fight and had plenty of them.

Their personalities, too, were at opposite ends of the scale. Ezra was the proud and self-centered teacher, convinced he was right about everything, never willing to open up his deepest feelings. Williams, in turn, was a humble, if at times bitter, follower of his friend's instructions about what to read, whom to publish; and much less certain there was in fact one and only one answer to any given problem. Williams was a purely emotional being, who took a personal point of view on every experience.

Ezra might have said, over and over, that "only emotion endures," and when it came to his own poetry, he certainly *wrote* by that rule; but he did not, like his doctor friend Bill Williams, *live* by it.

Pound sailed for Genoa aboard the liner *Cristoforo Columbo*. From there, he went to Schloss Brunnenberg, near Merano, where he lived for a year with his daughter, Mary, her husband, Prince Boris de Rachewiltz, and their two children, Pound's grandchildren. Then, ever restless, ever the poet in motion, he returned once again to Rapallo.

For several years in the early 1960s, Ezra Pound—who, throughout his life, never seemed to be finished saying all he had to say, to all the people he knew—withdrew into a vow of silence. Only his piercing, angry, and, perhaps, regretful eyes, revealed the absolute attention he gave his visitors. His last *Canto*, number 120, reads:

> *I have tried to write Paradise*
>
> *Do not move*
> *Let the wind speak*
> *   that is paradise.*

> *Let the Gods forgive what I*
> *have made*
> *Let those I love try to forgive*
> *what I have made*

In old age, like his friend in Rutherford, Ezra Pound begged forgiveness. He died in Venice, on November 1, 1972.

~§

"As Ezra says," Williams told a friend, late in life, recalling yet another important piece of advice from the master, "The poet must always be writing, even when he has nothing to write about—just for discipline."

And so it was with the epic poem, *Paterson*. Williams at first planned a carefully built work in four books, ending with the mighty Passaic pouring into the sea. It was the river of time, "our home whither all rivers/run . . . ," he declared, "You will come to it, the blood dark sea/of praise. You must come to it."

Finished? No, Williams could not accept the message in his own eloquent words. Instead, he pushed on into *Paterson V*. The city and the river needed a poet to keep them from dying in the pollution and economic decay of the twentieth century. And equally, this poet needed his disciplined work on the poem to keep him from giving in to deadly idleness. The fifth book was published in 1958.

The story of Paterson, as city and poem, would come to an end only when the author ceased to strive. "Dance, dance!" the ailing William Carlos Williams pleaded with himself and drove himself onward as he sketched rough notes for *Paterson Book VI* in January, 1961, "loosen your limbs from that art which holds you faster than the drugs which hold you faster." He would dance, as he insisted in a poem he wrote about the Russian astronaut, Yuri Gagarin, the first man to orbit the earth, "Heel and toe to the end." Williams, too, would dance the stubborn dance of words in the heaven of his imagination.

And he would dance because his grandchildren asked Williams—their "Pop-pops"— to write poems. He was inspired by his newfound love for the kids.

He nicknamed Suzanne, Paul's daughter, "Butter Ball." They spent such happy hours at the cottage at the shore in West Haven, Connecticut, where as a young girl, she pranced in the water, naked and carefree. "Your grandfather/is a poet and loves you," he wrote to her,

> *a bunch of violets clutched*
> *in your idle*
> *hand gives him a place*
>
> *beside you which he cherishes.*

When Paul Williams and his wife, Virginia, were going through a lengthy and painful divorce, Suzy took it hard. Williams was there to comfort her.

Paul, Suzy's older brother, was—true to Williams family tradition—a fanatic about trees. Before Williams's eyesight failed, grandfather and grandson spent hours driving around Rutherford surveying the varied foliage. Every time Paul spotted a different kind of tree, he insisted upon leaping out of the car, to measure its circumference. "Pop-pops, please make up a little poem about my pet turtle," Paul begged him. Williams replied gladly, in verse, "When we are together/you talk of nothing else,"

> *The turtle lives in the mud*
> *but is not mud-like,*
> *you can tell it by his eyes*
> *which are clear*

Paul never let go of his loving memories of "Pop-pops," years later naming his own son, Paul Carlos Williams.

Emily, Elaine, and Erica, William Eric's three eldest daughters, likewise received parting gifts in poetry from their proud grandfather. "When I first witnessed/your head/and held it," he told baby Erica,

> *admiringly between*
> *my fingers*
> *I bowed*
>
> *my approval*
> *at the Scandinavian*
> *name they'd*
>
> *given you*

Like the unicorn, the mythical, proud, fabulous beast Williams had seen woven into a medieval tapestry, its noble white body surrounded by a gilded fence, the poet spent the final year of his life as his mother had, caged in, blind, at home.

He waited anxiously for the publication of a final collection of poems, *Pictures from Breughel*, listening for the postman's steady tread up the front steps each morning. "I'm dying to live to see that book come out," he told James Laughlin, "I hope, I hope I make it." A copy arrived in June, 1962. It was Williams's forty-eighth book since the first slim volume, *Poems*, in 1909.

"Bill fades slowly and steadily," Flossie wrote, with resignation, to a friend that July, "He can't read—can't talk distinctly—and his memory is just nonexistent. It's sad to witness the collapse of a personality that was so vital, energetic, and humane. Such is life."

Williams and Flossie celebrated their fiftieth wedding anniversary on December 12, 1962.

William Carlos Williams had once written of his hope to pass away in peace in his bed. On the morning of

March 4th, 1963, he died of a cerebral hemorrhage at Nine
Ridge Road, in his sleep.

~§

The day of the funeral service was windswept, gray, and
rainy. The funeral parlor was crowded, solemn Ruther-
fordians pressed shoulder-to-shoulder with mourning poets.
In his eulogy, the Unitarian minister, Donald Curry, spoke
of William Carlos Williams's full and generous life as
"Ol' Doc," the man most of them knew. But he also reminded the townspeople of a fact they still might not have
realized: the world had now lost a great writer who had
lived among them.

At the grave in Hillside Cemetery, under a tent set
up against the rain, Reverend Curry read Williams's poem,
"Tract:"

> *I will teach you my townspeople*
> *how to perform a funeral . . .*
> > *sit openly—*
> *to the weather as to grief.*
> *Or do you think you can shut grief in?*

Suddenly, the clouds passed, the sky cleared, and the
sun shone.

CODA:

"I come, my sweet,
to sing to you"

May 14, 1973. I drove slowly, slowly down Ridge Road toward the center of Rutherford, looking to the right and left for Number Nine. Beside me in the front seat of the car were a window-box of purple pansies, and a freshly-bound copy of my Ph.D. dissertation; two big, black volumes, the complete catalogue of William Carlos Williams's papers at Buffalo.

I was here at last, on my first visit to Rutherford. A quiet place, a country kind of quiet, that afternoon in spring. Huge trees arched high above. As I moved downhill, light filtering through leaves made bright, flickering patterns on the windshield. There was a heavy, pungent smell of cut grass in the air. Carefully-arranged flower beds decorated well-trimmed lawns. Children rode by on tricycles. Mothers pushed baby carriages. A long, low church appeared at my left, just before the intersection. "That must be Park Avenue," I thought, "where all the shops are."

And there it was, *his house*, on a slight rise above street level, dull yellow in color, looming much larger than I'd imagined, partly hidden by trees and shrubs. I parked

196

the car, cradled my books in one arm, balanced the pansies in the other, mounted the steps leading to the front door, rang the bell, and waited.

Flossie knew I was coming. James Laughlin had telephoned her the day before, said she should expect me about four in the afternoon. I looked at my watch. It was just four now. I was nervous. Would she know who I was? Would she invite me in? Would she like me? And what should I *say* to her?

I rang the bell again. Silence. The occasional chirp of a bird, somewhere around the side of the house. Had she forgotten? I half-turned and stepped back, then rang the bell again, waiting, as so many before me had waited, so many writers, friends, admirers, newspaper reporters, patients.

Sounds of shuffling feet. The heavy door opened slightly. "Yes?" A vigorous, pleasant voice, a low voice, drifted from the shadows. "Mrs. Williams," I said, "It's me. Neil Baldwin." Florence Williams was a woman of eighty-three, a slight, fine-boned woman with stark white hair. A flower-print house dress hung loosely over her thin body. She wore thick glasses, and hearing aids in both ears.

She extended her hand to me. I grasped it; warm, dry, the long, slender fingers gnarled from arthritis, the grip sure and firm. "Come in, come in." She smiled and peered up at me, "Jimmy Laughlin told me all about you! Come in!"

Flossie led me through a dark entranceway into the long front room, sat me down close to her on the couch, put her hand gently, weightlessly on my knee, and reminded me to speak directly into her left ear.

"Do you like pictures?" she asked, motioning me to walk around the room, directing me to look first at a pastel by Marsden Hartley, then a delicate painting by Charles Demuth ("Poor man; diabetic, you know, and one of Bill's closest friends. So many of his friends were artists."). I saw a huge canvas given to Williams by Ben Shahn, an original Audubon engraving, and a Charles Sheeler painting.

On the mantel above the fireplace at one end of the room were several photographs of Flossie and Williams together, another of Williams striding along beneath trees, wearing a seersucker jacket, his straw hat at a jaunty angle. Flossie's writing table stood covered with papers. Above it, in a glass-fronted display, all her husband's books were arranged in neat rows. Through an archway, I glimpsed the dining room; a polished table shone at its center.

"Go on upstairs and you'll find Bill's study," she urged me from her spot on the couch, "I'll wait for you here." I entered a dim room, inhabited by a desk with an electric typewriter shrouded upon it, a cot, and not much else except, on an armless chair, a dusty cardboard box filled with condolence letters. I stood still for one long moment, listening to the quiet of the years, and the quiet of his room, which had for so long echoed with the noise of writing.

"Oh, how Bill *hated* that electric machine—but after the stroke, he was forced to use it," Flossie said, her voice rising, as I rejoined her. She spoke with regret of her confinement. "I can't go out too much, anymore," she said sadly, "Bill and I used to travel all over together . . . now, I watch too much television and think too much. He was a *great* guy, a great doctor . . . You would have liked him . . . He would have liked you. Bill just *loved* to talk with young people . . ." She turned toward me. The afternoon light flashed off her glasses.

I gave her the pansies. She was delighted. "How did you know? I *love* flowers!" I laughed to myself, thinking of countless flower poems, of the lush garden in back of the house. She ran her fingers lightly over the little blooms, caressing them, "Got to keep pinching these back all the time. You mustn't let pansies crowd together too much, or they'll die," she said.

A pause. Flossie leaned back into the cushions. "I'm getting tired, so tired . . . you'll have to go. Thank you for driving out here—and just to see *me*!"

I felt as if I had hardly spoken to her. But what

would I have said, even if the words had come? Should I have told her that I knew she was her husband's loving protector and steadfast booster; his strong-willed helpmate for his whole writing life? Should I have told her that anyone who admired William Carlos Williams's poetry must also in equal fashion admire her?

She walked me to the front door. We shook hands and said a simple good-bye. I eased into the car and looked back, up to the doorway. Flossie was standing there still, a fragile figure, waiting and watching. I waved—had she seen me wave to her one last time?—and the front door of Nine Ridge Road closed, slowly.

Three years later, Florence Herman Williams died at home, in the early morning hours of May 19, 1976, in the same room where she had given birth to her two sons.

Source guide for quoted material

xxvi : "the artist is" Dijkstra, *Art & Artists*, p. 199.
"all writing" *SE*, Preface, p. iv.

p. 5 : "of mixed ancestry" *Letters*, to Horace Gregory,
July 22, 1939.

6 : "No man ever" *Auto*, p. 15.

7 : "Behind him . . . later 1870s" *YMW*, p. 116.

8 : "a romantic" *YMW*, p. 33.
"The Spanish have" *YMW*, p. 47.

9 : "Gentle Jesus" *IWP*, p. 2.

10 : "Oh boys keep" *Auto*, p. 4.

11 : "A red rose" *YMW*, p. 127.
"Profound detail" *Auto*, p. 19.

13 : "Underneath it all" *Letters*, to Flossie, September 28,
1927.

14 : "I wasn't licked . . . I flew" *Auto*, pp. 26–27.

16 : "Put foot!" *YMW*, p. 14.
"What makes one" *Auto*, p. 48.

18 : "Beauty is truth" Keats, *Poems*, p. 82.
"You'll never be" *Auto*, p. 45.

19 : "Words offered themselves . . . wide berth" *Auto*,
p. 48.

20 : "didn't intend to" *Auto*, p. 51.

23 : "I was introduced" *Letters*, to his mother, December 9, 1902.

24–25 : "I have always" *Letters*, to his mother, November 8, 1904.

25 : "Well, if you're interested" Wagner, *Interviews*, p. 9.

25 : "the livest" *Auto*, p. 58.

26 : "was like B.C. and A.D." *IWP*, p. 5.

27 : "Not one person" *Letters*, to his mother, March 30, 1904.

"bread . . . caviar" Wagner, *Interviews*, p. 81.

"Writing has parts" *SE*, Preface.

28 : "When I was inclined" *IWP*, p. 4.

"I celebrate myself . . . in me" Whitman, *Poems*, p. 25 ff.

29 : "You have done" *Auto*, pp. 54–55.

31 : "Carlos, Carlos" Farnham, *Demuth*, p. 48.

32 : "She is tall" *Letters*, to Edgar Williams, April 12, 1905.

33 : "She's a girl" *ibid*.

"Your father is" *WCWN*, II.2, Fall 1976, p. 2.

34 : "loose-limbed beauty" *Letters*, to Edgar Williams, Apr. 12, 1905.

"feet always seemed" *Im*, p. 12.

"Come, beautiful rain" *Auto*, p. 69.

35 : "There is another trolley" H.D., *Torment*, p. 12.

36 : "a little book" *ibid*., p. 69.

"Child of the grass . . . rain" *ibid*., p. 68.

"a lady tall" *ibid*., p. 73.

"Mr. Pound" *ibid*., p. 17.

37 : "I call her" *Letters*, to Edgar Williams, March 11, 1906.

"I'm dead in love" *Letters*, to Edgar Williams, May 6, 1906.

38 : "Remember, you are" *Letters*, to Edgar Williams, March 18, 1906.

41 : "To do what" *Letters*, to Edgar Williams, November 12, 1906.

42 : "One thing that" *Letters*, to Edgar Williams, October 21, 1908.

43 : "Happy melodist . . . On sale now" Wallace, *Bibliography*, pp. 7–9.

44–45 : *"Poems composed" ibid.*, p. 9.

45 : "Look, Ez" *Auto*, p. 91.

"You'd better come" Pound, *Letters*, February 3, 1909.

"Individual, original" *ibid.*, May 21, 1909.

46 : "Why do you" *BU*, p. 238.

"Tell Charlotte . . . I'll go" *BU*, p. 258.

47 : "straight legs" *ibid.*, p. 201.

"take him as he was" *ibid.*, p. 262.

49 : "Bo, this country" *Letters*, to Edgar Williams, August 11, 1909.

50 : "I will not yield" Whittemore, *Williams*, p. 68.

52 : "I bless the muscles" excerpt from Williams's notebook, 1914, courtesy of William Eric Williams, M.D.

53 : "These are the great" *FD*, p. 331.

54 : "I'm proud, too" *BU*, p. 309.

55 : "No, not while" *Auto*, p. 128.

57 : "I'm a *great* poet" *Letters*, to Harriet Monroe, March 5, 1913.

"I only wish" *Letters*, to Viola Baxter Jordan, October 30, 1911.

"to sound like the sea" Wagner, *Interviews*, p. 63.

58 : "bold, heavily-accented" Pound, *New Freewoman*, December 1, 1913.

"built up as " *ibid.*

59 : "The hard sand breaks" Robinson, *H.D.*, p. 33.

62 : "He'll come with" *BU*, p. 317.

63 : "It's a bear!" Mariani, *Williams*, p. 112.

75 : "Don't bother to come" *Intrepid*, David Ignatow interview with Florence H. Williams, Spring 1974.

77 : "Went madly in" *Auto*, p. 135.

78 : "What were we seeking?" *ibid.*, p. 148.

"Don Quixote" Guimond, *Williams*, p. 13.

79 : "Strive for precision" Moore, *Reader*, p. 273.

80 : "the leading light" *Letters*, to Marianne Moore, February 21, 1917.

"willingness to be reckless" Moore, *Reader*, p. 273.

"Happening to stand" Moore, *Poems*, pp. 38–39.

"To get a book" *Auto*, p. 159.

83–84 : "The moon is low . . . without him?" *FD*, 208.

84 : "Welcomed the feel" *FD*, p. 142.

85 : "to write whatever" *Im.*, p. 13.
"So far away" *ibid.*, p. 34.

86 : "How smoothly" *ibid.*, p. 36–37.
"This is a slight" *ibid.*, p. 73.

87 : "The one thing" *Auto*, p. 159.

87–88 : "He's gone" *Auto*, p. 166.

88 : "You know all that" *Auto*, p. 14.

89 : "an age of miracles" Churchill, *Decade*, p. vii.

90–91 : "the poet puts" *IWP*, p. 32.

91 : "My head is" *CEP*, p. 196.

94 : "We, *Contact*" *SE*, p. 28.

94–95 : "citizens of the world" *SE*, p. 35.

95 : "so in place" *Letters*, to Marianne Moore, December 23, 1919.

95–96 : "You make my" *Letters*, to Marianne Moore, March 23, 1921.

96 : "Two-gun Williams" Baldwin, *Catalogue*, p. 235.

99 : "They are us" *Auto*, p. 236.

99 : "the local causes" *IAG*, p. 219.

100 : "deliberately chose" *IAG*, p. 131.
"the mountains were" *ibid.*, p. 132.
"commonness, his humble" *IAG*, p. 153.
"maligned because of" *IAG*, p. 192.

101 : "insane doggedness" *IAG*, p. 16.

102 : "Paris! its frivolity" *VP*, p. 13.
"the Paris of" *Auto*, p. 190.
"Williams seemed lost" McAlmon, *Geniuses*, p. 166.

103 : "Oranges, mandarins, lemons" *Letters*, to Marianne Moore, February 10, 1924.

104 : "ripe center" *Letters*, to Kenneth Burke, March 26, 1924.
"had heard" *VP*, p. 178.

105 : "I am not" *VP*, p. 240.

106 : "shapes, foliage, trees" *VP*, p. 263.

108 : "to find an image" *Pat*, p. 6.
"the concept of" *ibid.*, p. 7.

110 : "Once a man" Williams, New York Times *Book Review*, Jan. 15, 1950.

113 : "a big, serious" *Descent of Winter*, October 23, 1927.
114–115 : "Get that first one" *FD*, p. 250.
117 : "I think of my Bunny" *Letters*, to Flossie, September 25, 1927.
118 : "the spray from" *ibid.*
"old bean going around" *Letters*, to Flossie, September 26, 1927.
"for some uncanny" *Letters*, to Flossie, September 28, 1927.
"lash and slash" *Letters*, to Flossie, September 30, 1927.
122 : "Ring, ring, ring" *Im.*, pp. 275–76. Written January 11, 1929.
126 : "a shape which" Wagner, *Interviews*, p. 25.
127 : "I take what" *ibid.*, p. 25.
"No one believes" *ibid.*, p. 16–17.
137 : "I live where I live" *Letters*, to Kenneth Burke, 1932.
138 : "rid of medicine" *Letters*, to Kenneth Burke, January 26, 1933.
"the secret gardens" *Auto*, p. 288.
139 : "Doctor, you fix" *ibid.*, p. 124.
"a tough little nut" *ibid.*, p. 119.
141 : "Death is difficult" *FD*, p. 221.
142 : "each time they awake" *WM*, p. 171.
"Carry on" *IWP*, p. 61.
"curled up in the center" *ITM*, p. 105.
143 : "her little eyes" *BU*, p. 19, 22.
"We've got to move" *ibid.*, p. 35.
"Mother nature" *WM*, p. 212.
144 : "Everyone wants" *ibid.*, p. 138.
146 : "Here's something" James Laughlin, conversation with the author, September 29, 1982.
148 : "Bill, the older" *Letters*, to Marsden Hartley, Fall 1932.
"You seem not far . . . speak of humor" *Letters*, to William Eric Williams, March 13, 1935.
150 : "What should the artist" *SE*, p. 196.
"after a while" *ibid.*, p. 197.
151 : "not just with regard" Pound, letter to Francis

Biddle, Attorney General of the United States, August 4, 1943, in Cookson, ed., *Selected Prose*, pp. 14–15.

"to protest" *ibid.*

152 : "acquired a habit" *Letters*, to James Laughlin, June 7, 1939.

154 : "puffs of white cloud" *Auto*, p. 13.

155 : "ol' Doc Williams" *Auto*, p. 316.

"Are you a loyal" *Auto*, p. 318.

"the blameless leader" *SE*, p. 138.

"he *was* a friend" *Letters*, to McAlmon, January 19, 1943.

155–156 : "You are not going" Pound, in Norman, *Casebook*, pp. 40–41.

158 : "Is it not a crime" *Letters*, to Robert McAlmon, Feb. 23, 1944.

158–159 : "A father follows" *Letters*, to William Eric Williams, July 12, 1944.

161 : "And there was a smell" Pound, *Canto LXXIV*.

165 : "I feel ashamed" *Letters*, to Ezra Pound, July 1, 1946.

166 : "*Never explain anything*" Williams, in Norman, *Casebook*, p. 49.

167 : "longed-for time" *Letters*, to Wallace Stevens, April 25, 1951.

169 : "very food and drink" *Auto*, p. 357–58.

170–171 : "Take the oyster" Wagner, *Interviews*, p. 77.

171 : "Why does every line" 1954 Tape recordings, Rutherford Free Public Library.

"What is poetry" *ibid.*

"But this language of yours" *Auto*, p. 311.

172 : "Let everyone answer!" Whitman, *Poems*, pp. 394–95.

172–173 : "The first thing" *Auto*, p. 387.

179 : "Yes, I do understand" Kenneth Burke, conversation with the author, July 27, 1982.

183 : "approaching/death" *Paterson*, p. 269.

185 : "He reminds me . . . if he'll be up again" Robert Creeley, conversation with the author, November 11, 1982.

187 : "I know you will" *Pat*, p. 205.

191 : "I have tried" Pound, *Cantos*, p. 803.

192 : "As Ezra says" Wagner, *Interviews*, p. 75.

193 : "Pop-pops" Paul H. Williams, conversation with the author, October 26, 1982.

194 : "I'm dying to live . . . make it" James Laughlin, lecture at Donnell Library, New York City, February 25, 1982.

"Bill fades slowly . . ." Flossie to Oscar Silverman, July 3, 1962, in Whittemore, *Williams*, p. 350.

Bibliography

The works of William Carlos Williams

*(All books are published in paperback
by New Directions Publishing Corporation, New York,
unless otherwise indicated.)*

Collected Earlier Poems, 1951.* (*CEP*)

Collected Later Poems, 1963.* (*CLP*)

Paterson, 1963. (*Pat.*)

Pictures from Breughel and other poems, 1962. (*PB*)

Selected Poems, 1968. (*SP*)

Autobiography, 1967. (*Auto.*)

The Build-up, 1968. (*BU*)

The Embodiment of Knowledge, edited by Ron Loewinsohn, 1974. (*EK*)

The Farmers' Daughters, Collected stories, 1961. (*FD*)

Imaginations, edited by Webster Schott, 1971. (*Im.*)

Interviews, "*Speaking Straight Ahead*," edited by Linda Wagner, 1976. (*Int.*)

In the American Grain, 1956. (*IAG*)

In the Money, 1967. (*ITM*)

I Wanted to Write a Poem, reported and edited by Edith Heal, 1978. (*IWP*)

Kora in Hell—Improvisations. San Francisco: City Lights Books, 1967. (*Kora*)

Last Nights of Paris, translation of novel by Philippe Soupault, New York: Full Court Press, 1982.

Many Loves, Collected plays, 1965. (*ML*)

The William Carlos Williams Reader, edited by M. L. Rosenthal, 1966.

A Recognizable Image, William Carlos Williams on Art and Artists, edited by Bram Dijkstra, 1978. (*Image*)

Selected Essays, 1969. (*SE*)

Selected Letters, edited by John C. Thirlwall. New York: McDowell, Obolensky, 1957.* (*Letters*)

Spring & All, New York: Frontier Press, 1970. (*Spring*)

A Voyage to Pagany, 1970. (*VP*)

White Mule, 1967. (*WM*)

Yes, Mrs. Williams: A Personal Record of My Mother, 1982. (*YMW*)

Tape recordings at the Rutherford Free Public Library:

March 26, 1954, NBC "Anthology" show interview.

March 28, 1954, NBC "Collector's Item" interview.

June 18, 1954, "Voice of America" interview.

(*available in hardcover edition only)

Selected general reading

ALLEN, DONALD M., and WARREN TALLMAN, editors. *The Poetics of the New American Poetry*. New York: Grove Press, 1973.

BALDWIN, NEIL, and STEVEN L. MEYERS. *The Manuscripts and Letters of William Carlos Williams in the Poetry Collection of the Lockwood Memorial Library, State University of*

New York at Buffalo, A Descriptive Catalogue. Boston: G. K. Hall & Co., 1978.

BROOKS, VAN WYCK, editor. *The American Caravan.* New York: The Macaulay Company, 1927.

CHURCHILL, ALLEN. *The Literary Decade.* Englewood Cliffs, NJ: Prentice-Hall, Inc., 1971.

COLES, ROBERT. *William Carlos Williams, The Knack of Survival in America.* New Brunswick, NJ: Rutgers University Press, 1975.

DE RACHEWILTZ, MARY. *Discretions, Ezra Pound, Father and Teacher.* New York: New Directions, 1975.

DOOLITTLE, HILDA (H.D.). *Bid Me to Live.* New York: Grove Press, 1960.

————. *End to Torment, A Memoir of Ezra Pound.* New York: New Directions, 1979.

————. *The Gift.* New York: New Directions, 1982.

————. *Hermetic Definition.* New York: New Directions, 1972.

————. *HERmione.* New York: New Directions, 1981.

————. *Selected Poems.* New York: Grove Press, 1957.

DUBERMAN, MARTIN. *Black Mountain, An Experiment in Community.* New York: E. P. Dutton & Company, 1972.

EDEL, LEON. *Literary Biography.* Bloomington, IN: Indiana University Press, 1973.

ELIOT, T. S. *Selected Prose.* New York: Harcourt Brace Jovanovich, 1975.

ELLMANN, RICHARD, editor. *The New Oxford Book of American Verse.* New York: Oxford University Press, 1976.

ELLMANN, RICHARD, and ROBERT O'CLAIR, editors. *The Norton Anthology of Modern Poetry.* New York: W. W. Norton & Co., 1973.

FARNHAM, EMILY. *Charles Demuth: Behind a Laughing Mask.* Norman, OK: University of Oklahoma Press, 1971.

FEDERAL WRITERS' PROJECT OF THE WORKS PROGRESS ADMINISTRATION OF THE STATE OF NEW JERSEY. *Bergen County Panorama.* Hackensack, 1941.

————. *New Jersey, A Guide to its Present and Past*. New York: Hastings House, 1939.

FLANNER, JANET. *Paris Was Yesterday*, 1925–1939. New York: Viking Press, 1972.

FLEMING, THOMAS. *New Jersey, A History*. New York: W. W. Norton & Co., 1977.

FORD, HUGH. *Published in Paris*. New York: Macmillan, 1975.

GINSBERG, ALLEN. *Howl and Other Poems*. San Francisco, CA: City Lights Books, 1959.

GUIMOND, JAMES. *The Art of William Carlos Williams*. Urbana, IL: University of Illinois Press, 1968.

HARRISON, GILBERT A., editor. *Gertrude Stein's America*. New York: Liveright, 1974.

HENDERSON, BILL, editor. *The Publish-It-Yourself Handbook*. Yonkers, NY: Pushcart Press, 1973.

HOLLAND, NORMAN. *Poems in Persons*. New York: W. W. Norton & Co., 1973.

JARRELL, RANDALL. *Poetry and the Age*. New York: Vintage Books, 1955.

KEATS, JOHN. *Selected Poems*. New York: Appleton-Century-Crofts, 1950.

KENNER, HUGH. *The Counterfeiters*. New York: Anchor Press, 1973.

————. *The Pound Era*. Berkeley, CA: University of California Press, 1971.

LAUGHLIN, J., editor. *New Directions in Prose and Poetry*, No. 17. New York: New Directions, 1961.

LAWRENCE, D. H. *Studies in Classic American Literature*. New York: Viking Press, 1964.

LYNCH, KEVIN. *The Image of the City*. Cambridge, MA: MIT Press, 1960.

McALMON, ROBERT. *Being Geniuses Together 1920–1930*. Revised by Kay Boyle. London: Michael Joseph, Ltd., 1970.

MARIANI, PAUL. *William Carlos Williams, A New World Naked*. New York: McGraw-Hill Book Co., 1981.

MAZZARO, JEROME. *William Carlos Williams, The Later Poems.* Ithaca, NY: Cornell University Press, 1973.

MOORE, MARIANNE. *Complete Poems.* New York: Macmillan/ Penguin, 1982.

————. *A Marianne Moore Reader.* New York: Viking Press, 1972.

NORMAN, CHARLES, editor. *The Case of Ezra Pound.* New York: The Bodley Press, 1948.

PLIMPTON, GEORGE, editor. *Writers at Work, The Paris Review Interviews, Third Series.* New York: Penguin Books, 1979.

POUND, EZRA. *The ABC of Reading.* New York: New Directions, 1960.

————. *The Cantos.* New York: New Directions, 1973.

————. *Literary Essays.* Edited by T. S. Eliot. London: Faber and Faber, 1963.

————. *Selected Letters.* Edited by D. D. Paige. New York: New Directions, 1971.

————. *Selected Poems.* New York: New Directions, 1957.

————. *Selected Prose.* Edited by William Cookson. New York: New Directions, 1975.

PREMINGER, ALEX, editor. *Princeton Encyclopedia of Poetry and Poetics.* Princeton, NJ: Princeton University Press, 1974.

REXROTH, KENNETH. *American Poetry in the Twentieth Century.* New York: Seabury Press, 1973.

RICHARDS, I. A., editor. *The Portable Coleridge.* New York: Viking Press, 1950.

ROBINSON, JANICE S. *H.D.: The Life and Work of an American Poet.* Boston: Houghton Mifflin Co., 1982.

ROSE, BARBARA. *American Art Since 1900.* London: Thames & Hudson, 1967.

ROSENFELD, PAUL. *Port of New York.* Urbana, IL: University of Illinois Press, 1966.

SEELYE, CATHERINE, editor. *Charles Olson and Ezra Pound, An Encounter at St. Elizabeths.* New York: Viking/ Grossman, 1975.

SIMPSON, LOUIS. *Three on a Tower*. New York: William Morrow & Co., 1975.

STEIN, GERTRUDE. *The Autobiography of Alice B. Toklas*. New York: Vintage Books, 1960.

STOCK, NOEL. *Reading the Cantos*. New York: Minerva Press, 1968.

SUTTON, WALTER. *American Free Verse*. New York: New Directions, 1973.

TASHJIAN, DICKRAN. *William Carlos Williams and the American Scene 1920–1940*. New York: Whitney Museum of American Art, 1978.

TOMLINSON, CHARLES, editor. *William Carlos Williams*. Harmondsworth, Middx.: Penguin Books, 1972.

VAN O'CONNOR, WILLIAM, and EDWARD STONE, editors. *A Casebook on Ezra Pound*. New York: Thomas Y. Crowell, 1959.

WALLACE, EMILY MITCHELL. *A Bibliography of William Carlos Williams*. Middletown, CT: Wesleyan University Press, 1968.

WEAVER, MIKE. *William Carlos Williams, The American Background*. Cambridge: Cambridge University Press, 1971.

WHITMAN, WALT. *Complete Poetry and Selected Prose*. Boston, MA: Houghton Mifflin Co., 1959.

WHITTEMORE, REED. *William Carlos Williams, Poet from Jersey*. Boston, MA: Houghton Mifflin Co., 1975.

Articles

BALDWIN, NEIL. "Discovering Common Ground: A Note on William Carlos Williams and Valery Larbaud," *American Literature*, 45.2, May 1973.

———. "The Stecher Trilogy: Williams as Novelist," *William Carlos Williams, Man and Poet*. Edited by Carroll F. Terrell. Orono, ME: National Poetry Foundation, 1983.

———. "The World It Opens: William Carlos Williams' 'The Descent'," *Ordinary*, I.1, 1977.

————. "Zukofsky, Williams, and *The Wedge*," *Louis Zukofsky, Man and Poet*. Edited by Carroll F. Terrell. Orono, ME: National Poetry Foundation, 1979.

DE LOACH, ALLEN, editor. "Bill Williams and Flossie's Special," *Intrepid*, 39–41, 1980.

MARIANI, PAUL, editor. "A Garland for William Carlos Williams," *Massachusetts Review*, XIV.1, Winter 1973.

RATZAN, RICHARD, MD. "No Wreathes Please: For William Carlos Williams," *Annals of Internal Medicine*, 97, 1982.

WILLIAMS, WILLIAM CARLOS. "Seventy Years Deep," *Holiday*, XVI.5, November, 1954.

William Carlos Williams Newsletter, I.1 (Fall, 1975)— V.2 (Fall, 1979); title changed to *WCW Review*, VI.1 (Spring, 1980)—present.

Poems by
William Carlos Williams
quoted in text

(Asterisk indicates entire poem is quoted.)

INDEX

NEIL BALDWIN, Distinguished Visiting Professor in the College of the Arts at Montclair State University, is the critically acclaimed author of many works of biography and nonfiction, including *The American Revelation* and *Henry Ford and the Jews*. He is co-chair of the New York University Biography Seminar, and served on the Program Committee for the 2008 Annual Meeting of the Organization of American Historians. His website is www.neilbaldwinbooks.com and his occasional blog on education and culture is www.nj.com/njvoices.